A Sense of Siege

The Geopolitics
of Islam and the West

Graham E. Fuller
and Ian O. Lesser

Westview Press

BOULDER • SAN FRANCISCO • OXFORD

A RAND Study

RAND books are available on a wide variety of topics. To receive a list of Rand books, write or call Distribution Services, RAND, 1700 Main Street, P.O. Box 2138, Santa Monica, CA 90407-2138, (310) 451-7002.

Published in 1995 in the United States of America by Westview Press, Inc., 5500 Central Avenue, Boulder, Colorado 80301-2877, and in the United Kingdom by Westview Press, 12 Hid's Copse Road, Cumnor Hill, Oxford, OX2 9JJ

A CIP record for this book is available from the Library of Congress.
ISBN 0-8133-2148-4—ISBN 0-8133-2149-2 (pbk.)

Printed and bound in the United States of America

The paper used in this publication meets the requirements of the American National Standard for Permanence of Paper for Printed Library Materials Z39.48-1984.

10   9   8   7   6   5   4   3   2

Contents

Preface

This book, the result of an exploratory project conducted by the authors within the Strategy and Doctrine Program of RAND's Arroyo Center, builds on a number of related RAND research activities touching on Middle Eastern, European, and Central Asian topics. Our findings incorporate the results of extensive discussions with official and unofficial observers in the United States and abroad. We wish to thank all of the individuals who contributed their views over the course of our research, as well as those who have been instrumental in supporting this effort at RAND. In particular, we are most grateful to James T. Quinlivan, Vice-President for RAND's Army Research Division and Director of the Arroyo Center, Bruce Hoffman and Mary Morris, respectively Director and Associate Director of the Center's Strategy and Doctrine Program, and Cynthia Kumagawa of the RAND Book Program. We are also indebted to Benjamin Schwarz at RAND and Augustus Richard Norton of Boston University for their extremely useful critiques. Finally, our thanks go to Barbara Kliszewski and Rosalie Heacock at RAND for their invaluable assistance in editing the manuscript.

The authors are especially pleased to note that this book is also being issued under the auspices of RAND's new Greater Middle East Studies Center, based in Santa Monica and Washington.

1

INTRODUCTION

In one sense, there is no "Islam," and there is no "West." These terms are abstractions we readily use, but in the end they mean quite different things to different people at different times and under different circumstances. It is the goal of this book to discern just what we are—and are not—talking about when referring to the "problem of Islam and the West."

Indeed, it has become fashionable since the end of the Cold War to speculate that the next ideological struggle in the world may be between "Islam" and "the West." This speculation is founded on the belief that there must of necessity be a next "ism" that will challenge Western societies. This proposition is not entirely groundless: The kind of symbolic and real power represented by the West—and the United States in particular—in the cultural, political, economic, and military arena is formidable and intrusive. Almost by definition the West's global presence is bound to generate some kind of counterresponse.

The reality of a powerful West perhaps strikes Muslims more vividly than it strikes the West itself. It is a presence and power against which all other calculations must be gauged when Muslims operate in the international arena or even formulate certain kinds of policies at home. It was for just this reason that the collapse of the Soviet Union made most Third World countries uncomfortable—not because of any special love for the old communist order, but simply because the sudden disappearance of Moscow from international politics limited the options of smaller nations, now forced to navigate in international waters dominated by a single superpower or a Western bloc of power. If we examine the current ideological spectrum and the gaping hole once occupied by the Soviet Union, it is not unreasonable to suppose that some kind of geopolitical and ideological counterweight—or combination of counterweights—will inevitably emerge to correct this strategic imbalance, to fill the vacuum left behind by the implosion of the Soviet counterweight to Western power.

But will Islam fill this vacuum? We use "Islam" here in quotation marks simply because there is no Islam per se that can be treated as a single,

1

cohesive, coherent, comprehensive, monolithic entity. There are various sources of Islamic theology and law, including the Quran, the sayings of the Prophet (Hadith), religious laws by extrapolation (*ijtihad*), and other articles of faith, and traditional practices. In addition, there are Sunni and Shi'ite branches of Islam, (each of which has broad and diverse subdivisions), a variety of schools of theology, a wealth of Sufi or mystical brotherhoods, regional customs, and differing historical personalities and experiences among dozens of Muslim countries across three major continents and a complete spectrum of climates that collectively serve to make up "Islam." Thus Islam will never constitute a single entity. Needless to say, the concept of the West is at least as diverse.

Why should Islam be so often popularly perceived as the political and ideological rival to the West? Many reasons suggest themselves. The long history of religious confrontation between the two great neighboring religions of Christianity and Islam goes back thirteen centuries—even though that relationship has hardly been characterized by confrontation alone. There is a more recent history of Western imperialism and colonialism in most Muslim countries, the legacy of which has not been forgotten in the Muslim world, even if Western powers today view it as a bygone, irrelevant in contemporary terms.

Islam is probably more deeply integrated institutionally into state and society than any other comparable religion. This gives it greater staying power as a cultural force distinct from the West and renders it more impervious to the inroads and assaults of Westernization.

Islamic "fundamentalism" (an imprecise and poor term for analytic purposes) has been the single most anti-Western force over the past two decades, especially with the withering away of communism. Muslim states have, furthermore, offered the West several dramatic "hate figures" unparalleled almost anywhere else in the world: Gamal Abdel Nasser, Mu'ammar al-Qadhafi, the Ayatollah Khomeini, and Saddam Hussein among the most arresting examples in Western demonology.

With the collapse of communism, no other coherent set of beliefs dispersed among people over a wide geographic area has emerged to pose a systematic critique of the West as strongly and clearly as has radical Islam. At the same time, the Middle East has represented the single most frequent venue for Western military intervention over the past few decades, even more so when Israel itself is regarded as a Western power in the Middle East, both in character and backing.

Like it or not, Islamic societies will have to face the realities of the dominance of a Western-centered international order of capitalism, free trade, nation-states, democratization, and human values that corresponds to Western patterns of development. There is no alternative world in which Islamic societies can live unless they wish to consign themselves to complete marginality. This reality does not mean, however, that the Western-constructed order will not be subject to reform, change, and calls for greater responsiveness to the needs of other societies. This process of change can take place only through working from within the system rather than from outside.

In simplest terms, then, Islam has evolved in the minds of many observers as the next most likely candidate of opposition to Western interests across much of the globe. In the eyes of some observers, this perceived struggle between "Islamic" and "Western" interests has come to take on the character of a conflict between two great differing systems of civilization.[1]

Although only a few serious analysts pose the problem of Western relations with Muslim states in such starkly polarized terms as "Islam versus the West," the expression has achieved a certain currency both in the West and in the Middle East, primarily on the extremes of the political spectrum. The concept of Islam versus the West is taken seriously enough internationally to require examination by policy makers. For all the talk about it, are there, in fact, issues that can in any way be characterized as Islam versus the West? Or is it an ill-founded concept?

Significant questions arise in attempting to resolve this debate. What are the *concrete* issues between Islam and the West that create the perception of a broader confrontation? What is the basis of existing frictions? Does the existence of frictions mean that they must necessarily merge into a grand ideological confrontation? Under what circumstances do a mixed set of practical bilateral problems take on broader cultural overtones, lending them civilizational, global, and ideological weight? What conditions of political and economic crisis might facilitate broader demonization of both Islam and the West—much as the Nazis were able to suggest that the ills of Germany flowed from the Jews, or Soviet communists could suggest that the capitalists were the source of world ills? Lastly, how might these frictions best be managed to limit the mutual damage?

To anticipate some of our key conclusions: First, we do not believe that relations between Islam and the West per se represent the arena of the next global ideological struggle. Islam as a faith is not on a collision course with the West. The issue is not between Christianity and Islam. There does exist, however, a whole series of specific, discrete issues of a bilateral nature between individual Western countries and Muslim countries that requires close attention. As perhaps the preeminent symbol of conflicting regional interests, Islam may inevitably be drawn into the center of much North-South discourse. More generally, Third World aspirations are going to place increasing demands upon advanced nations for constructing relationships of greater equity and dignity of treatment. Failure by Western states to accommodate them will encourage Third World radicalism in both its nationalist and Islamist expressions. Gross mishandling of political relationships on both sides can broaden the ideological aspect of confrontational relationships and could well lead to the consolidation of states into opposing blocs.

Second, political Islam will seek to enhance the real power of Muslim states—a goal not unique to Islamist politicians—in their relations with the stronger West in order to deal from a position of greater equality rather than strategic weakness. This will imply a search for greater military power, including weapons of mass destruction, in order to equalize relations with the West, at least in the strategic arena. Again, these goals are hardly unique to Islamist leaders.

Third, the role of Islam is likely to grow in the internal politics of Muslim countries. Only by exposure to and inclusion in the political process will Islamic politics eventually lose its current attraction and become more normal. Because the phenomenon of political Islam is being mishandled by a number of important Muslim states, the chances of Islamists coming to power in one or more Middle Eastern countries over the next several years are good.

A fourth and central theme of this book concerns the urgency of political, economic, and social change away from old authoritarian orders in the Middle East. It is political Islam that most threatens the established order in most Muslim countries—far more than it threatens the West itself. Utilizing the grievances produced by the old order, political Islam pursues an agenda that seeks power and the overthrow of the status quo. We believe that this "threat"—and it is real to many authoritarian regimes—can ultimately be managed only through co-option and inclusion of Islamist forces to one extent or another within the political system. Exclusion will most likely lead to growing confrontation and possible explosion. But the process of successfully integrating Islamists into the political system is complex and tricky. Mishandled, it can lead to considerable destabilization of the political order. No solution is simple or easy, because the forces that evoke violence and radicalism are not readily contained.

The formulation "Islam and the West" embraces a range of deeply rooted historical and psychological perceptions. This legacy has been augmented by a complex assortment of modern developments, including the legacy of decolonization, the distortion of Western policy toward the Third World during the Cold War, international terrorism, oil concerns, and Western intervention in regional crises. Whereas we do not propose to explore all the differences that have emerged between "Islam and the West," we do need to identify at least the range of issues that serve as the sources that create friction and affect attitudes.

Our goal, then, has been to disentangle—to separate and clarify—the problems that arise between the Muslim world and the West in general. We believe that formulating this issue in "Muslim-Western" terms is neither particularly descriptive nor accurate, nor does it represent a constructive or even effective approach to the genuine issues that do exist between the West and the Muslim world. A sweeping "civilizational" approach can even be harmful over the longer run, not so much because it is false in all cases but because that kind of emotive characterization leads to simplistic and damaging views by both sides, a recipe for self-fulfilling prophecies. By placing these problems in a more objective context, we hope to offer some possible avenues for alleviating, if not overcoming, specific policy problems affecting relations between Islam and the West.

But to return to the conundrum posed at the outset, what is "Islam"? Or for that matter, what is "the West"? Are these ideal terms for policy analysis? We think not. They are too broad in character, embracing diverse regions of the world and a mixture of different cultures, attitudes, and perceptions. Yet they are hardly meaningless terms either because in moments of confrontation "Islam" and "the West" sum up images of what provokes one or the other party. Nor do these concepts operate solely at the high, policy-making levels. The seizure of Western hostages by "Muslims" or the bombing of Muslim peoples by Western warplanes evoke powerful emotions at the popular level on both sides and lead to equally powerful pressures on policy makers, with serious consequences.

For purposes of this book the term "Muslim" includes all who believe in and practice Islam or who consider themselves to be Muslim in a cultural sense, part of a Muslim society whether practicing or not. "Muslim" as an adjective refers to states that either possess a Muslim majority or consider themselves to be Muslim, but not necessarily "Islamist." "Muslim" in this sense also refers to the broad range of cultural practices of Islam across the globe from Africa to East Asia; it is largely interchangeable with the term "Islamic," in every case associated with the religion of Islam.

Much of this book is also concerned with the phenomenon of Islamic "fundamentalism." The term is a misleading one, particularly because it is borrowed from Protestant Christianity and does not exist per se in the languages of the Islamic world, except for use in Western countries. Although in this study we occasionally use the term as a convenient catchall in reference to particular Western concerns, we prefer to avoid it when analyzing these movements. We prefer "Islamism" and "Islamists"—terms that do exist in the various languages of the Muslim world. Islamism can also be usefully called "political Islam," for it is Islam's political role that is the focus of greatest policy attention. Thus, while in theological terms the austere Wahhabi sect of Islam in Saudi Arabia is fundamentalist in its desire to return to basic principles of Islam, Islam as practiced daily in Saudi Arabia is not considered to be political Islam, because it does not enter into the political process per se. Even here, however, the practice of Wahhabi Islam has been politicized by a few radical groups and could be converted into political Islam as a contemporary movement—against the will of the Saudi people.

"Islamism" is a modern term for a basically modern phenomenon: political movements based on Islamic principles, usually not led by the clergy—who, in fact, often challenge the traditional clergy and their status quo outlook—interested in modern mechanisms of publicity and mobilization of the masses, in possession of a political agenda that usually goes beyond mere religious goals to seek the reform of state and society. These movements espouse political, economic, and social change, especially in the interests of the lower and lower middle classes of society.

Much of the existing and potential friction between Islam and the West does not necessarily involve political Islam per se. Confrontation can emerge as an expression of frustration or hostility from Muslims who are not specifically adherents of political Islam but who nonetheless possess grievances that influence their political behavior toward the West. In this study we are interested in any form of cultural or religious expression from the Muslim world that can be related to anti-Western feelings.

If defining "Islam" is difficult, defining "the West" is even harder—not just for Westerners but for Muslims as well. Sometimes to Muslims "the West" means the entire industrialized world, including Japan—that is, those who exert dominant influence over the international economy, such as the G-7 states. At times, "the West" means former colonial nations—all European— who conquered and dominated most of the Muslim world at some point in history. (Among significant Muslim states, only Afghanistan and Saudi Arabia lack this colonial experience.) On other occasions, "the West" actually refers to the United States as the leading Western power and dominant political, cultural, and economic actor in the Muslim world. Even here, whose America is being talked about? Is it simply U.S. government policy, or is it American culture that has evolved largely independent of the state? And what of the large numbers of Americans who are Muslim (now approaching the second largest religious group in the United States), or those Americans whose roots in a variety of Third World states that may cause them to identify with some of the grievances of the Third World as a whole? Lastly, "the West" can refer to elements of Western populations who hold and express negative impressions of the Muslim world en bloc. Clearly there is no single coherent "West" opposed to Muslim countries, any more than there is a single "Islam" expressing hostile views toward the West.

We have employed the phrase "Islam and the West" in the subtitle of the book with some misgivings. In an earlier age this study might more appropriately have been entitled "Islam and Christendom" or "the Muslim versus the Judeo-Christian world." Indeed, to some Muslims that is precisely what we are talking about. Is the problem primarily a theological one—an inherent doctrinal irreconcilability? Or are we pitting distinct historical religious communities, states, and their interests against each other? Despite efforts by some observers to find cultural dissonance rooted in theological-juridical origins, we do not believe tensions between Islam and the West are theological in nature. The critical differences are political, economic, psychological, strategic, and cultural, springing from the two great civilizations that have emerged from these two world faiths.

As a matter of fact, most Westerners, however religious they may be, do not really think of themselves primarily in terms of being Christian.[2] Indeed, the concept of Christendom to most Westerners is redolent of the Middle Ages and thus almost antiquated in its implications. But to Muslims who still possess a concept of community in Islam (the *umma*), the term "Christendom" is perhaps still meaningful as the mirror image of the *umma*.[3] Indeed, some unworldly Muslims continue to think of the medieval Christian opponent in the original religious terms rather than in the much broader civilizational sense represented by the term "West" today. Finally, to some Islamists a central problem of the West is precisely that it has abandoned its religious and moral ideals, many of which are quite compatible with Islam. Instead, Western populations who once thought of themselves primarily as Christians have created a secular, modern culture that in Muslim eyes is now conspicuous for its seeming absence of Christian or moral principles in personal behavior; it is precisely the export of this seeming Western amorality that constitutes a perceived cultural threat to the traditional principles of the

Muslim community.

In a sense, the relationship between Islam and Western Christianity is ambiguous precisely because, of all faiths, these two religions are the most universal in character, both in their extraordinary pervasiveness and in their doctrines in which ethnicity is entirely absent as a formal concept. Eastern Christianity in its various forms is in fact closely linked with ethnicity, whether Greek, Armenian, Romanian, Russian or Serbian Orthodox, Coptic, or Assyrian. This link at one time constituted one of the deep sources of hostility and schism between Eastern and Western Christianity, Byzantium and Rome. Finally, in much Islamic polemic "the West" also includes Israel, not on religious grounds, but because modern Israel is perceived as the intellectual creation of Jews from Europe and is linked intimately with the West in political, cultural, economic, and strategic terms.

We devote special attention to the "fault line" that runs geographically between the Islamic world and the Christian world, starting with the Mediterranean—across which Muslims and Westerners view each other—southward into Africa, up through the Balkans, across the Caucasus, and on into Central Asia where Islam faces Russia. The study devotes less attention to South Asia and Southeast Asia, where there is also an "Islamic fault line," but not, of course, generally bordering on Christian cultures. Nonetheless, the intensity of the Hindu-Muslim confrontation contains some characteristics reminiscent of the Western-Muslim problem and we briefly touch upon it.

We anticipate the objection from some that by dissecting the nature of issues at stake between Islam and the West along functional lines, we are in effect attempting to make the problem go away. Those observers would argue that the whole of the problem is greater than the sum of its parts. Bernard Lewis thus claims that "we are facing a mood and a movement far transcending the level of issues and policies and the governments that pursue them. This is no less than a clash of civilizations."[4] Some will prefer to reject treatment of the various component elements of the problem in preference for more emotive discussion of "clash of cultures" that almost by definition are beyond description or analysis and therefore defy treatment.

Civilizations are indeed real, powerful, and complex forces. Rather than the cause, they are vehicles for grievance and solace in times of crisis. But we cannot accept that we are dealing with forces beyond identification and remedy, including in the perceptual and psychological areas. Our approach, then, differs fundamentally from that of those who choose to cling apprehensively to the specter of an inevitable, deterministic clash; we look instead to analysis of understandable and perhaps partially manageable grievances and conflicts of interest. If civilizations will always to some extent remain mysterious and impenetrable to one another, the actual gap between Islamic and Western culture is probably less than that between Western and Hindu, Western and Japanese, or Western and African cultures.

The first section of this study is devoted to historical and psychological perceptions between the (Muslim) East and the West. Relations between the two regions and civilizations carry immense historical baggage, much of which persists in the recesses of local memory today, especially when resuscitated as contemporary grist for an ideological mill. This section is divided into two parts: the Western perception of Islam, and the Muslim perception of the West. Both have their own mirror visions of history, myths, perceptions, and potent images. Yet we are not speaking of two sides equally (ill-)informed about each other. On the contrary, the preponderance of Western media and Western activity on the international scene has made Muslim awareness of Western attitudes, values, and fears far deeper than the relatively limited Western exposure to the anxieties, grievances, and aspirations of the Muslim world.

Section 2 of the study looks at the contemporary policy dilemmas facing the two sides, concrete points of friction, and contrasting perceptions of national interests and goals. Among other things this section examines issues such as terrorism, refugees, oil supply policies, Western military intervention, weapons proliferation, and trade policies. Note that many of these issues are not specific to Muslim-Western relations but involve a range of concerns and grievances between the West and the Third World as a whole. Like the first section, this section is divided into two: First are considered dilemmas posed to the West by the Muslim world; second, dilemmas posed by the Muslim world to the West.

Section 3 examines the religious dimension. First, to what extent might Islamic doctrines of propagation of the faith (expansionism) and *jihad* (holy war) predetermine conflict with the West? Second, what are the prospects for Islamic solidarity for common purpose, including against the West? Finally, this section also examines the phenomenon of Muslims living in the West, beyond the migration issue. What is the potential impact of the Muslim diaspora on future relations between the two cultures? Does the presence of Muslims in the West lead to greater understanding or greater friction? What effect does Muslim life in the West have on the evolution of Muslim thinking in general? We suggest that the experience of Muslims in the West may be an important indicator of the kinds of changes Muslim societies in the Middle East and elsewhere will experience in the future.

Section 4 examines the strategic dimension. We examine potential flash-points along geopolitical fault lines, the borderlands between Muslim and non-Muslim regions, and how they might evolve. We also ask whether there are differing "strategic cultures" in the Islamic world and the West. To what extent can the two regions reach agreement on matters of security and stability? Here, too, we attempt to analyze the degree to which these issues can be approached as diverse and discrete, dealt with individually, rather than thrown together in an emotive and undesirable ideological context.

Section 5 provides some concluding observations and suggests policy implications for the United States. The first essential political task for policy makers is to avoid the facile temptation to see the problem as immutable, involving an inexorable clash of civilizations. However intriguing cultural conflicts may be to students of culture, this approach at a policy level is simply a "cop-out." Although cultural differences unquestionably exist, a bleak belief in the inherent incompatibility of the cultures offers nothing by way of solution and even plays at the fundamentalists' own game by furthering the image of an unquestionably hostile West.

Both authors spent much time together in attempting to reach a common outlook on the problems examined in this book. Some differences of view and emphasis do exist, and we did not avoid them here. The analytical and writing task was divided as follows, roughly reflecting our respective interests and expertise. The Muslim historical view of the West (Chapter 3), the Muslim perception of their current grievances (Chapter 5), the religious aspect of the problem (Chapter 6), the prospects for Muslim solidarity (Chapter 7), and the geopolitical dimension (Chapter 8) have all been explored by Graham Fuller. The West's historical view of the Muslim world (Chapter 2), the West's current concerns with regard to the Muslim world (Chapter 4), and differences in strategic culture (Chapter 9) have been addressed by Ian Lesser. The introduction and conclusion were jointly written. Both authors have critiqued and informed the views of the other.

Lest the discussion of these issues become too theoretical and discursive, it is worth stressing here the questions foremost in the authors' minds throughout this effort:

1. What are the key issues at stake in conflicts between specific Muslim and non-Muslim states that are unrelated to Islam per se? Are these problems growing or diminishing?
2. How much is Islam itself a factor in conflict between countries that are Muslim and those that are non-Muslim? What factors or scenarios might be likely to

decrease or increase the degree to which Islam is seen as a leading element on either side?

3. To what degree is Islamic solidarity likely to grow? Around which issues might it coalesce? What policies would it adopt toward the West? Conversely, what factors serve to weaken Islamic solidarity, worsening the prospects for joint action?

4. What are the key factors that in cultural/religious terms complicate the relations of Islamic states with the West?

5. What is the experience of Muslims abroad? To what extent are they becoming secularized or having a secularizing effect on Muslim states?

6. What policy recommendations can we make to prevent regional and functional conflicts from taking on the characteristics of a broader confrontation with Islam?

Some readers, especially in the Islamic world, may feel that the very title of the study, the very treatment of the theme, encourages the concept of an unbridgeable divide between Islam and the West. Similarly, some may see this study as a blueprint for furthering the struggle for Western power and influence over the Muslim world. The authors categorically reject any such intent. Indeed, both of us are deeply committed to the concept of reconciliation and cooperation between civilizations. We believe that careful examination of the problem will establish useful terms of discussion and contribute to intelligent policy debate within and between the Western and Muslim worlds.

Although no one side is more right than the other, the kinds of accommodations that need to be made on both sides are often quite different. While mutual understanding is laudable, serious policy issues do exist between both sides that require equally serious thought in the quest for solutions. The issue of the imbalance of power is one of the most complex, for the perception of inequality invariably complicates relationships of any kind. If this study is able to lessen casual and sensationalist references to a new cold war and to set an agenda for issues to be addressed by both sides—with a better understanding of the psychological baggage in the way—much will have been accomplished.

Notes

1. This thought has been most dramatically formulated in Samuel Huntington, "The Clash of Civilizations?" *Foreign Affairs,* Summer 1993.

2. A significant exception may be the Eastern Orthodox Christians, for reasons to be discussed later.

3. Indeed, while visiting a mosque in Kokand, Uzbekistan, I spoke with the local mullah, who raised this very question. After I had queried him for half an hour about the condition of Muslims and Islam in Kokand since the collapse of communism, the mullah looked at me suspiciously and said, "Wait a minute. Aren't you Christian? Then why have you spent half an hour talking about the Muslim community and have not asked me one single question about the condition of the Christian community around here?"

4. Bernard Lewis, "The Roots of Muslim Rage." *Atlantic Monthly,* September 1990, p. 24.

2

WESTERN HISTORICAL PERCEPTIONS OF ISLAM AND THEIR GEOPOLITICAL LEGACY

The relationship between Islam and the West now occupies center stage in the post–Cold War debate over the future direction of international affairs. But the issue itself is a very old one, with powerful and enduring images flowing from historical experience and perceptions on both sides. The West— and here we are referring largely to Europeans—has been exposed to Islam virtually since its inception, and Muslim societies have been the subject of scholarly and diplomatic study since the Middle Ages. Historically, the West has known, or thought it has known, a great deal about Islam, and certainly much more than the Islamic world has known about the West.[1] This asymmetry of knowledge and interest was apparent throughout the great period of European-Ottoman confrontation and characteristic of the relationship through the end of World War II and beyond. The situation may now be reversed with the increasingly global dissemination of Western media. The average urban Moroccan or Turk will have some view about American or French society and politics. Few Americans would be as well informed about developments in Rabat or Ankara. The Western public tends to pay serious attention to developments in the Muslim world only as a result of crises affecting Western interests. The Gulf War provided a striking example of this. At least for Europeans, the turmoil in Algeria provides another.

Although U.S. interaction with the Muslim world did not begin in earnest until the early nineteenth century, images derived from centuries of European experience are an important part of the intellectual approach to Islam on both sides of the Atlantic. A full treatment of the history of relations between Islam and the West is obviously beyond the scope of this study and has, in any case, been covered with great expertise by a variety of scholars. Nonetheless, some essential themes are worth exploring because of their close connection to contemporary perceptions.

Europe and Asia

The Western view of Islam has always been closely connected to the definition of "foreign." Today, as in the fifteenth century, the first foreign (i.e., non-European) culture one encounters moving south or east from Europe is Islam. European interaction with its Asian and Mediterranean periphery has been a dominant factor in the evolution of the continent's own sense of its geopolitical position and world role. Indeed, the distinction between Europe and the lands to the east as a basis for political and strategic analysis predates the arrival of Islam on the world scene. In what is arguably one of the first and most enduring geopolitical assessments, the ancient Greeks developed a strong sense of the geographic and cultural distinction between Europe and Asia and saw their most potent strategic competitor in "Asiatic" Persia.[2] The rise of Byzantium and the schism between East and West within the Roman Empire and Christianity reinforced the perception of civilizational "frontiers." Thus by the time of the great Islamic conquests of the seventh and eighth centuries the notion of the cultural and strategic competition between Europe and Asia was already a well-established tradition in European thought. In this schema the lands on the European periphery and the Mediterranean itself were seen as a barrier, a defensive glacis in an enduring struggle between civilizations.

The modern West tends to associate the Muslim world with the Middle East, or what eighteenth- and nineteenth-century Europeans called the Orient. But until the retreat of Ottoman Turkey from Europe, the Orient was widely seen as beginning where Hapsburg influence ended in the Balkans. Much of what Europeans conceived of as the Muslim world—areas under Ottoman domination even if largely Christian—existed within the geographic confines of Europe. With the reawakening of Muslim identity in the Balkans as result of the war in Bosnia and the reemergence of religious activity suppressed under communist regimes, Europeans are once again confronting an uncomfortable historical legacy. As at least one observer has pointed out, post–Cold War developments in this region may compel a fundamental reassessment of how we define "Europe" and the "Middle East."[3] An important point of interaction between Europe and the Muslim world has been reestablished, with a range of potential consequences, positive and negative.

Islam and the Loss of Mediterranean Unity

The experience and perception of a strong cultural divide between Asia and Europe, Islam and the West, has thus been an important part of the European world view. It is not the only tradition relevant to contemporary problems, however. A potent alternative tradition has emphasized the existence of a historic common heritage and civilization around the Mediterranean linking southern Europe, North Africa, and the Levant. This heritage is the legacy of the Roman Empire and its more or less unified system of cultural, political, and economic relations between north and south, east and west across the Mediterranean. It is a system that persisted long after the loss of Roman administration and which was finally broken by the extension of Islam and Arab power westward across North Africa in the eighth century. The insecurity that the rapid series of Muslim conquests brought to southern Europe, and the resulting loss of free communications not only between north and south but, above all, between east and west played an important role in the development of Europe through the Middle Ages. A prominent school of historiography has been established around this "loss of Mediterranean unity" and the negative and enduring consequences for Europe and relations between Europe and the Islamic world. For European historians in the mold of Henri Pirenne, the rapid advance of Islam was the pivotal event leading to the intellectual and political break with the traditions of antiquity. "The Western Mediterranean, having become a Musulman lake, was no longer the thoroughfare of commerce and of thought which it had always been. . . . The West was blockaded and forced to live upon its own resources."[4]

Islam itself can be viewed as the last of the great Mediterranean civilizations with a unifying thrust.[5] The confluence of Islamic political movements across North Africa and the Levant, and the growing prominence of the Islamic factor in the Balkans, suggests that Islam's potential as a unifying force in the Mediterranean region is far from over. All too familiar with the artificiality of states created as a result of decolonization, many European observers readily find unity of purpose in the actions of Islamic countries to the south and east. Movements such as the Arab Maghreb Union (AMU), viewed with some skepticism in Arab capitals, are taken more seriously across the Mediterranean, especially by those Europeans hoping to reestablish a sense of Mediterranean unity. Western European initiatives for regional security and cooperation, including the Conference on Security and Cooperation for the Mediterranean (CSCM) and the "Five plus Five" consultations reflect a desire to open a Mediterranean dialogue through agreement on essentially Western standards of respect for human rights, inviolability of borders, and so on.[6]

Islam in Europe and Insecure Borderlands

For almost a millennium the Islamic threat was the main strategic problem for Europeans from Iberia to Austria and the Balkans, and beyond if Russia and the period of the "Tatar yoke" is included. In retrospect it is difficult to perceive the full extent and potency of this threat, which made itself felt in local as well as grand strategic terms. The defeat of the Moors at Poitiers in 732, the Turks at Lepanto in 1571 and again at Vienna in 1683 have achieved a certain canonical status as defining moments in the conflict between Islam and the West for control of European territory. The significance of these Western victories lies substantially in the perception that they were "close-run things." Without dismissing the advantages of geography, military technology, and political organization that may have worked in Europe's favor—and European superiority increased steadily with time—there has been a powerful and enduring perception that at times the fate of Europe has hung in the balance. The image of the Turks "at the Gates of Vienna" as late as the seventeenth century has become a fixture in contemporary Western analyses of revived Muslim-Christian cleavages. Edward Gibbon in *The Decline and Fall of the Roman Empire* speculated that if Charles Martel had been defeated at Tours or Poitiers, the Quran "would now be taught in the schools of Oxford."[7]

The process of Europe's own expansion since the fifteenth century is closely tied to the conflict with Islam. After the long struggle to end Muslim occupations from Spain to Russia and to reestablish Christian rule in areas where important Muslim civilizations had taken root, "it was hardly to be expected that the triumphant Spaniards and Portuguese would stop at the Straits of Gibraltar, or that the Russians would allow the Tatars to retire in peace and regroup." This Western counteroffensive beginning in the fifteenth century was given additional impetus by concurrent Turkish expansion into European territory in the Balkans, an advance to the Danube threatening Central Europe itself.[8] The age of European maritime exploration and the colonial expansion in Asia and across the Atlantic paralleled the reconquest of Spain. In particular, the opening of the Cape Route by the Portuguese led to the progressive outflanking of Ottoman power in the eastern Mediterranean, which had previously impeded direct European access to trade with the East (and which had also forced a good deal of commercial contact between the Ottoman Empire and the West). The spirit of the Crusades and reconquest was carried forward to a degree in the early European voyages of exploration, where the principal opponents of Portuguese penetration around the Indian Ocean were, again, Muslim principalities.

The reconquest of Muslim territories in Spain has left an enduring legacy in the western Mediterranean, where the yearning for past greatness is felt on both sides of the Straits of Gibraltar. Indeed, the debate over the meaning of the reconquest in cultural and geopolitical terms has long been an important part of the intellectual scene in Spain, with revisionist interpretations gaining strength since the end of the Franco era. In recent years the rediscovery of Spain's Moorish heritage based on the Almoravid, Nasrid, and Umayyad dynasties, which flourished from the ninth to the fifteenth centuries, has become pronounced in certain circles and has even led to a minor interest in Islamic religious practice and culture.[9] The experience of the reconquest remains a source of deep ambivalence in Spain, where the wider confrontation with Islam in the form of the Ottoman Empire continued long after the capture of the last Moorish stronghold in Granada in 1492. Centuries after the "expulsion" of Islam from Spain, it should not be surprising that Spanish public opinion regards the growing influx of Muslim migrants from North Africa with concern. The modern Spanish language abounds with archaic references to the conflict with the Moors.

Perhaps as significant as the conquest and reconquest of the Iberian Peninsula or the advance of Ottoman power in the Balkans was the prolonged experience of European insecurity in the face of Muslim raids and periodic occupation of points along the northern Mediterranean coast.[10] In the Barbary states, Morocco, and the Ottoman-controlled principalities of Algeria, Tunisia, and Tripolitania, a sea-borne *jihad* remained in force in the western Mediterranean long after the principal era of conflict with Ottoman power had ended. North African "piracy" was a reality affecting commerce and European security through the end of the eighteenth century and was a catalyst for the establishment of U.S. naval power and diplomacy in the Mediterranean in the early years of the nineteenth century.[11] The resulting fear of Muslim-inspired violence is deeply rooted in the European psyche, especially in the borderland regions that were especially vulnerable to these predations. The analogy to contemporary concerns about international terrorism and its close association with Middle Eastern affairs and Islamic radicalism in Western perception is noteworthy.[12]

The First Cold War

The new attention to relations between Islam and the West after the end of the East-West competition has suggested to many observers the possibility of a new Cold War along confessional lines. The potential for a new Cold War requires critical examination. But the use of this imagery is striking, not least since the extended competition between the West (Spain) and Islam (the Moorish dynasties and later Ottoman Turkey) was described by contemporary Spanish observers as a *guerra fría*, i.e., a cold war between cultures, perceptions, and arms that continued regardless of the outcome of individual battles.[13] The cold war analogy applies equally to the broader competition between Islam and the West in historical terms. After more than 800 well-documented years of conflict and coexistence with Islam on land and sea around the Mediterranean basin, Europeans came to perceive that although "mutually tolerable, even agreeable terms of accommodation are possible in social and intellectual matters," irreconcilable differences exist in the realms of political organization and warfare.[14]

A later aspect of the *guerra fría* tradition involved the Western view of Islam, here in the form of Ottoman Turkey, as an obstacle to modern nationalist aspirations in the Balkans and elsewhere. British, French, and U.S. support for Greek independence in the early 1800s was based on a potent combination: romanticism about the Greek legacy together with a desire to assist in lifting the cloak of "Ottoman ignorance and oppression" in the Balkans. The central role of the Orthodox Church in the leading Balkan nationalist movements has lent special significance and durability to religious cleavages as a feature of nationalism in the region, with obvious echoes in the current situation in the former Yugoslavia, Albania, and Bulgaria.[15] The perceived conflict between Islam and modern nationalism was also a feature of British and French interaction with the Arab areas of the Ottoman Empire prior to and during World War I. Indeed, this was to emerge as a central tenet of Ataturkism in post-Ottoman Turkey. Ironically, and despite the modern Western preference for national identity over religious identity, the Western experience with secular Arab nationalism in the period of decolonization and after would prove as uncomfortable as anything that had gone before.

The image of the struggle against Muslim domination is reemerging in the concepts articulated by Greeks, Bulgarians, Serbs, and Russians to describe their own security dilemmas, as well as their role in a post–Cold War European security system. The rise of a new (old) "Islamic factor" in Balkan and European security figures prominently in emerging debates in the region, with a special emphasis on these countries' critical position along a key civilizational and strategic fault line and their role as barriers to Islamic instability.[16] The degree to which this formulation finds some resonance in Europe as a whole is an open question. Certainly European thinking about Turkey's character and role has reflected a similar calculus about barriers to "Middle Eastern" instability. In the Islamic world, including Turkey, the perception that Western inaction in Bosnia derives in large part from European discomfort with an Islamic presence in the Balkans is pervasive. In the broadest sense the new debate over fault lines and the potential "clash of civilizations" has revived a very traditional emphasis on the special character of states on the European borderlands, the so-called *marca* states: Spain in the west, the largely Orthodox states of the Balkans, and Turkey in the east (in Samuel Huntington's formulation, a state "torn" between two civilizations).[17]

In the context of emerging political and security orientations in the Balkans, the potential for a "Muslim axis" composed of Turkey, Bosnia (or what remains of it), and Albania has received a good deal of attention.[18] The legacy of Islam in Europe arguably contributes to differences between Washington and its European allies on policy toward the crisis in Yugoslavia and, specifically, attitudes toward Bosnia. The emergence of a "Muslim-dominated" state in Europe has not been a matter of deep concern in U.S. policy circles, although there has been some fear of Iranian involvement. In Europe the prospect has given rise to substantial, if largely unstated, unease.[19] France and Russia have been in the forefront in this regard, but anxiety can be seen elsewhere. Moreover, attitudes toward Bosnia are developing against a background of broader concern about the political and economic crises along Europe's Muslim periphery, not least Algeria and Egypt.

The Legacy of Colonialism

A fundamental question for contemporary relations between Islam and the West concerns the extent to which current frictions are the legacy of religious and cultural conflict as opposed to the more recent experience of colonialism. The answer almost certainly lies somewhere between these two possibilities, with historical images from both sources interacting and, in many cases, reinforcing each other. Another open question concerns the potential significance of the absence of colonial "baggage" in America's relations with the Muslim world.

Interactions between European metropoles and colonial territories from the sixteenth century until well after 1945 were primarily interactions between the West and Islam. As a consequence, European interest in and knowledge of the Islamic world was, until the mid-1960s, strongly influenced by the requirements of colonial policy and the strains of decolonization. Moreover, European intelligence and practice with regard to Islamic affairs was motivated in large measure by great power competition on the European periphery and in Asia, with Ottoman weakness and the potential for Islamic revolt in India and North Africa as strategic wild cards. Thus, late-nineteenth-century Britain saw the maintenance of stable protectorates in Egypt and the Sudan as essential to safeguard communications with India, itself vulnerable to Muslim revolt. German strategists saw opportunities for influence across the Balkans and Anatolia and into Mesopotamia in a way that imposed increasing contact with the Muslim world and close relations with Ottoman Turkey.[20] Italy pursued imperial ambitions in Libya and the Horn of Africa; Spain maintained a colonial presence in northern Morocco and the Western Sahara. French possessions in North Africa and protectorates in the Levant played a central role in European power balances and imposed a high degree of contact with the Muslim world.[21] Thus the experience of colonialism and interactions between Europe and Islam are thoroughly intertwined. Just as the Orthodox-Muslim struggle in the Balkans played a leading role in the development of modern nationalism in that region, Islam played a leading symbolic role in anticolonial movements in Africa and Asia.

Although the colonial experience and the anticolonial conflicts are leading factors in contemporary Muslim perceptions of the West, the impact of these processes on European thinking, perhaps less obvious, cannot be ignored. Islam as a culture proved relatively resistant to colonial penetration, and Christian missionaries of the colonial era made few inroads in Muslim lands.[22] Europeans were quick to interpret this resistance as evidence of religious as well as political fanaticism, images reawakened by the often violent experience of decolonization.

The French perception of Algeria provides a striking example of this phenomenon. Unlike French territories elsewhere in North Africa and the Middle East, Algeria was regarded, and was in legal fact, a formal part of France. The cultural and economic ties between Paris and Algiers were, and to a surprising extent still are, numerous and profound. In strategic terms the security of Algeria was inextricably bound up with the security of France. The trauma of the Algerian revolution, which the Algerians compare with the revolutions of Russia and China, continues to produce echoes in French opinion, with displaced *pieds noirs* forming a key nucleus of support for the anti-immigrant right wing. The violence and perceived fanaticism of the Algerian nationalists as well as the *colon* reaction have not been forgotten.[23] French politicians and the foreign and security policy elite still have a special sensitivity to Algerian affairs, reinvigorated by the Islamic political challenge. The Algerian elite is similarly far closer in its approach to questions of politics and strategy to the French tradition than it is prepared to admit. Western observers of the turmoil in contemporary Algeria are aware that the Islamist challenge to the postcolonial political order is in many ways the reaction of traditional, rural Algeria (many of whose people now live in urban centers) to what is seen as the corrupt rule of a Francophile, Mediterranean elite.

The United States does not share in Europe's colonial legacy in North Africa or the Middle East. On the contrary, U.S. support for independence movements in North Africa after World War II remains an important source of goodwill in Algiers and elsewhere (and a still perceptible source of ill will in Paris).[24] But the United States does have a powerful reputation for intervention in the Islamic world, a reality that has made it difficult to capitalize on the anticolonial tradition in U.S. foreign policy. Moreover, intellectuals and political leaderships in the Muslim world, and the Third World in general, have tended to combine notions of colonialism, imperialism, and intervention in ways which cast the United States in a particularly unfavorable light. Nonetheless, at a time when Cold War concepts of nonalignment have lost much of their relevance, the question of the *divisibility* of past Western behavior toward the Islamic world may acquire new significance. With the changing international environment, historical images are likely to play a leading role in shaping Muslim views of the West, including the extent to which the West itself is seen as a uniformly antagonistic whole.

Recent Images: Suez, Oil, and the Iranian Revolution

To an overwhelming degree, relations between Islam and the West after 1945 were subsumed by the geostrategic and ideological competition with the Soviet bloc. Western concern about instability in Muslim regions was inextricably linked to the broader question of how Middle Eastern regimes might choose to advance or impede the containment of Soviet power. Even the apparently independent question of the Arab-Israeli dispute was overshadowed by considerations of Israel's strategic value in the eastern Mediterranean and the potential for superpower escalation as a result of regional crises. To the extent that relations with the Islamic world were considered in their own right, the focus tended to be on Arab nationalism rather than Islam per se and, not least, oil.

Several images from more recent experience have had particular salience in Western perceptions of the Islamic world. First, the series of events comprising the Egyptian revolution, the nationalization of the Suez Canal, and the subsequent Anglo-French intervention, against a background of colonial withdrawal and Soviet pressure, led to pronounced Western concern about the long-term geopolitical consequences of Arab nationalism. Second, the Arab oil embargo of 1973 and the supply crises of 1973–74 and 1981–82 gave rise to fears about the West's structural vulnerability to the "oil weapon" and supply interruptions as a result of regional instability or Soviet action. The Islamic factor was largely absent in both cases. The prevailing image was not one of impoverished and fanatical Muslims calling for the downfall of the West but that of wealthy "oil sheiks" holding the industrialized and many Third World economies to ransom and disposing of their petrodollars in a destabilizing manner.[25] Following the Soviet invasion of Afghanistan, Western observers tended to emphasize the nationalist character of the resistance forces. It was not until relatively late in the war that the *jihadist* aspects of the conflict became more widely known in the West. The apparent role of Afghani veterans in violent fundamentalist circles in North Africa and elsewhere suggests that arms and support provided to the movement throughout the 1980s was not an unmixed good. The Afghan experience has been interpreted by many people to be evidence of the basic irreconcilability of radical Islamic and Western approaches to international affairs, despite the occasional convergence of geopolitical interests.

A third, powerful image from recent experience derives from the Iranian revolution, the hostage crisis, and the continuing cold war with Teheran. Despite the awareness, certainly in expert circles, that Islam is hardly monolithic and that Islamic politics can take varied forms, there remains—especially in the United States—a concern that the Iranian model is more likely to be the norm rather than the exception where Islamic regimes come to power (e.g., on the pattern of Sudan). The image of revolutionary Iran, bolstered by developments such as the Salman Rushdie affair, overshadow much of the current U.S. debate about the rise of political Islam. It also makes it difficult for Americans to imagine relations with an Islamic regime in which the United States is not cast in the role of the "Great Satan."

The Gulf War, virtual Islamic revolutions in Algeria and Egypt, terrorist activities in the United States, and the Muslim dimension of the crisis in the former Yugoslavia have placed Islam at the center of U.S. and European foreign policy debates. This extraordinary attention to a single cross-cutting foreign and security policy issue has not been seen since the immediate postwar deliberations over the containment of communism. It has contributed to the perception that relations between Islam and the West have reached "a defining moment."[26]

Notes

1. The accuracy of Western intellectual images of the Muslim world and the character of potential biases are issues that been keenly debated. Edward Said offered a controversial critique of Western scholarship and literary portrayal of the Middle East in *Orientalism* (New York: Random House, 1978).

2. The early Greeks would not have sensed this distinction as clearly. For Homer there was no real distinction between Europe and Asia Minor; the Trojan War was not a conflict between East and West. But by the time of the Persian wars, and certainly by the time of Alexander's conquests, the cleavage between the Greek (i.e., European) and Oriental worlds was well developed. See Thierry Hentsch, *Imagining the Middle East* (New York: Black Rose Books, 1992).

3. See Robert Kaplan, "There is No 'Middle East,'" *New York Times Magazine*, February 20, 1994.

4. Henri Pirenne elaborated on this theme in *Mohammed and Charlemagne* (London: Unwin University Books, 1974), first published in 1939. A broader analysis of the factors that have united and divided civilizations around the Mediterranean is provided in Fernand Braudel's sweeping work *The Mediterranean and the Mediterranean World in the Age of Philip II* (New York: Harper & Row, 1973), first published in France in 1949.

5. As suggested by Maurice Aymard in a presentation to the Complutense University (Madrid) Summer Seminar, El Escorial, 1992.

6. Many observers remain profoundly skeptical about efforts to resurrect the "myth of Mediterranean unity." See, for example, John Chipman, "Mediterranean Security: What Bridges over What Troubled Waters?" paper presented at conference, "Security and Cooperation in the Mediterranean: Perspectives on the Future," sponsored by the Fundación Ortega y Gasset et al., Madrid, October 3–5, 1991.

7. See Bernard Lewis, *The Muslim Discovery of Europe* (New York: W. W.

Norton, 1982), p. 18; and William Pfaff. "Reflections: Islam and the West," *New Yorker,* January 28, 1991, p. 86.

8. See Bernard Lewis, *Islam and the West* (New York: Oxford University Press, 1993), p. 17.

9. See Alan Riding, "Cordoba Journal: As Ethnic Identity Grows in Spain, Pride in Islamic Roots Is Blooming," *New York Times,* March 1, 1993.

10. Raids as far afield as the English coast, though rare, were not unknown.

11. The Western relationship with the North African states was not exclusively confrontational. Both sides, as well as neutrals, found it convenient to establish agreements with local rulers during the Napoleonic Wars. See Lewis, *The Muslim Discovery of Europe,* pp. 45–47.

12. Lewis, *Islam and the West,* p.17.

13. See Adda B. Bozeman, *Strategic Intelligence and Statecraft: Selected Essays* (Washington, D.C.: Brassey's, 1992), pp. 235–255.

14. Ibid., p. 223.

15. See Sir Charles Eliot, *Turkey in Europe* (London: Frank Cass, 1965), first published in 1900.

16. See, for example, Oliver Potezica, "The Islamic Factor in the Balkans," *Review of International Affairs* (Belgrade), May–June 1993; "Serbian Politician on Islamic Fundamentalism," *JPRS-EER,* April 6, 1993, p. 49; and "Yugoslavia Discussed with Varvitsiotis," *FBIS-WEU,* April 9, 1993, in which the German defense minister, Volker Ruehe, reportedly stressed to his Greek counterpart the importance of opposing the expansion of an Islamic presence in Europe.

17. See Huntington, "The Clash of Civilizations?" The "civilizational" tensions in modern Turkish perceptions and policy are explored in Graham E. Fuller, Ian O. Lesser, et al., *Turkey's New Geopolitics: From the Balkans to Western China* (Boulder: CO: Westview/RAND, 1993).

18. F. Stephen Larrabee, "The Former Yugoslavia: Emerging Security Orientations," in Regina Cowen Karp, ed., *Central and Eastern Europe: The Challenge of Transition* (Oxford: Oxford University Press, 1993); see also Larrabee, *Turkey and the Balkans* (Ebenhausen: Stiftung Wissenschaft und Politik, 1993).

19. See Roger Cohen, "U.S. Clashes with Russia over Bosnia," *New York Times,*

May 18, 1994.

20. The confluence of German interest in Middle Eastern resources, the strategic potential of railways, and the opportunities for commercial and political influence in the East (the *Drang nach Osten*), was a persistent theme in German geopolitical thought from the mid-nineteenth century through World War II. It also gave rise to the abortive scheme for a Berlin-Baghdad Railway.

21. French contact with Islam had begun in earnest with Napoleon's expedition to Egypt.

22. Edward Mortimer, *European Security after the Cold War,* Adelphi Paper No. 271 (London: IISS, 1992), p. 36.

23. The scale of the violence during the revolution is often overlooked: Roughly one million casualties resulted among the Algerian population alone. See, for example, Alistair Horne, *A Savage War of Peace: Algeria, 1954–1962* (London: MacMillan, 1971).

24. During the negotiation of the NATO Treaty the issue of the geographic extent of the security guarantee, in particular whether or not French territory in North Africa would fall within the treaty area, was a significant point of contention between Paris and Washington. The treaty covers the Mediterranean, but only up to the North African shoreline; a fortuitous decision, given the French experience in Algeria a decade later.

25. In light of these perceptions, the financial difficulties currently facing the Saudi regime are all the more striking. See Stephen Engelberg et al., "Saudi Stability Hit by Heavy Spending of Last Decade," *New York Times,* August 22, 1993.

26. Robin Wright, "West Debates Muslim Surge," *Los Angeles Times,* April 6, 1993.

3

THE MUSLIM HISTORICAL AND PSYCHOLOGICAL PERCEPTION OF THE WEST

Two key themes most distinctly characterize the Muslim perception of its relationship with the West: the reversal of Islamic civilization's long preeminence and a broad sense among Muslims that they are under siege from the West and are operating from a position of weakness and vulnerability. These two concepts may surprise many in the West, who regard Islam as militantly self-confident and on the offensive. Yet not to grasp this psychological state of mind in the Muslim world is to miss a critical dynamic between the two regions.

Muslims are vividly aware of nearly 1,000 years of Muslim cultural, intellectual, scientific, technological, and military superiority that came to an end during the Renaissance. There followed a period of Muslim decline and European ascendancy that persists until today, during much of which time the newly dominant Europe came to impose its colonial and imperial power over the Muslim world. This chapter details the loss of Muslim greatness, the loss of power, and the loss of self-confidence.

The trauma of loss is intensified by a sense of internal decline and fracturing of a coherent Islamic civilization. An Islamic world with its established culture, law, norms, and values has given way over the past two centuries to penetration by Western culture; this penetration has sapped the coherence of Islamic civilization and forced it to conform in multiple ways to dominant Western power and civilization. The Muslim world has not fully accommodated itself to this profound shift in power relationships. Feelings of anxiety and insecurity lurk deep within the psyche of Muslim societies today, even if not expressly articulated as such. How does Islamic civilization reconcile its weakened and subordinate position in the contemporary world with the manifestation of God's favor bestowed upon the Islamic community ever since its vigorous and glorious flowering in the seventh century A.D.?

Islam historically views itself as the culmination of the history of God-given revealed religion on earth. Islam recognizes and reveres both Moses and Jesus as saints. But in the Muslim view Moses misunderstood God's message in believing that it was solely for Jews. Jesus understood that the message of the Old Testament was for all peoples, but in the Muslim view Christians proceeded to confuse Jesus with God: Instead of proclaiming Jesus a great prophet, which he was, they considered him literally the son of God. And God can be only one person in Muslim thought. As the last and greatest of the prophets Muhammad was the capstone of divine revelation, the final act in a series of prophetic missions in which the oneness of God was the central and final message. Islam was thus the most "universal," the most recent, and the most "final" of faiths. Unique to a world religion, Muhammad's mission also took place in the full light of history and was meticulously recorded, leaving little doubt as to what took place and what the message was in its every detail.

Muslims view the stunning spread of Islam, from Mecca to Gibraltar and Central Asia within one century, as a direct sign of God's favor. The long-sustained power of successive Islamic states was further testament to that favor. The mission of humans is understood by Muslims as the obligation to build communities that operate in conformity with God's laws as revealed in the Quran and the Prophet's words. Although many Muslim states have risen and fallen throughout history, one of the greatest Muslim empires, the Ottoman Turkish empire, did not reach collapse until the end of the nineteenth–early twentieth century—the last gasp of the extraordinary power of international Islam. Since that time the Muslim world has struggled to recreate past greatness in some way, but without success. Today the phenomenon of political Islam is partly a reaction to this decline, an effort to identify and correct the sources of Islamic weakness and to rediscover the roots of Islamic faith that can restore greatness, as manifested and measured by the strength of modern Muslim civilization and its societies.

If there is Muslim pain at the loss of greatness and the decline of power and influence, there is also mixed resentment and apprehension about the Western civilization that ultimately vanquished Muslim dominance. In Muslim eyes history, including modern experience, provides many grounds for grievance against the West. These grievances should be understood by Westerners from two points of view. First, it is important to recognize that there is a "Muslim version" of history that is very real to Muslims; it focuses on historical events important to the Muslim experience even if often ignored in Westerners' own version of history. Second, the Muslim reading of history places into context the psychological, cultural, and historical background of

Muslims' view of the contemporary world. Although Muslims may suppress active consideration of these historical events in their daily dealings with the West, such considerations are not absent in the their collective thinking. Suppressed for long periods of time, they can suddenly burst forth, seemingly "irrationally" in response to Western actions in the Middle East or elsewhere, evoking old concerns and fears. This study will not embark upon a recitation of Islamic history, but it will touch on several key issues in which Muslim interpretations and perspectives of history may be new to Western observers.

In reviewing a "Muslim interpretation of history" it is important to remember that history in cultural terms is far more than just a record of what happened. As all contemporary peoples reconsider their cultural and political heritages, selective aspects of the past take on new importance, retroactively revealing new perspectives perhaps missing at the time; history is continuously rewritten in the eyes of contemporaries according to their own needs and perceptions. Today, therefore, Islamist activists sift the Islamic past for the raw materials and historical grist for the conceptual and ideological mill of contemporary politics.

Islam as a Christian Heresy

The Islamic view of Christianity, then, is that after Jesus provided the world with important new revelations about the universality of Moses' message for all humans, Christians took a wrong turn in worshipping its messenger rather than God himself. In fact, apart from Jesus' claim to be the Son of God and the account of his resurrection, large parts of Christian and Jewish religious history are incorporated directly into Islam. Both Moses and Jesus are Muslim saints, as are large numbers of other Old Testament prophets. Thus there are some grounds for difference on the theological level—although hardly enough to create a "clash of civilizations" based on religious belief alone.

Christianity first seriously encountered Islam at the political level when expanding Islamic power in the seventh century met the Eastern Christian Byzantine empire based in Constantinople, which had extended at various times deeply into Middle East. Christians immediately viewed Islam as a Christian heresy.[1] The confrontation of Islamic and Byzantine power, which was to last nearly 800 years, was thus the beginning of a long power struggle couched in ideological terms between Muslim and Christian states, whose

Western locus shifted to western Europe after the fall of Constantinople to Islam in the fifteenth century.

The Crusades

Perhaps from the beginning Christianity and Islam were destined to be rivals as long as religion was the driving source of international relations.

> Those forces which first taught the world that the human race was one were indeed religious forces. The most universalist of all religions were the Semitic religions, especially Christianity and Islam. Precisely because Christianity and Islam wanted to convert every human being to their faiths, they were the most militantly globalist of all cultures.[2]

The arrival of Christian armies in the Holy Land on a pilgrimage and crusade from western Europe was just the beginning of a long-term general European campaign to recover territories under Muslim control in Spain, Sicily, the Levant, and elsewhere. Crusader forces over the course of 100 years seized and occupied nearly all of the Levant coast from the borders of Turkey to the borders of Egypt. Slow to react, by 1187 Muslim forces had finally eliminated the Christian Kingdom of Jerusalem and restored the region to Muslim control. But ever since, the Crusades have been a deeply emotional event for Muslims, representing not only the physical invasion of Western forces but the establishment of Christian states on Muslim soil as well. Today these events are retroactively seen as the forerunner of later Western colonialism and imperialism and, in the eyes of many Muslims, are linked to the establishment of a Jewish state in Palestine in 1948, conceived and led by Jewish immigrants from the West. Even though Christians and Muslims in the tenth and eleventh centuries were familiar with each other, and their communities lived together in most parts of the Near East, the Crusades symbolized the arrival of conquering armies in the name of religion. The Crusades might be viewed today in a far purer ideological light by Islamists than they ever were at the time, when power relations were more equal and cultural coexistence was commonplace in many areas.

The Reconquest of Spain

The Crusades marked the beginning of a broader military response by the Christian world to the successes of Muslim conquest in previous centuries. The Christian reconquest of Spain, in a centuries-long process from the eleventh to the fourteenth centuries, stands out in Muslim minds as the single most stunning and grievous loss. The word "Andalusia" still evokes in Muslim minds past greatness and glory, as well as deep sadness at the passing of one of the highpoints of medieval Islam. The 800 years of Muslim rule in Spain was one of the highpoints of civilization anywhere in Europe, with a rich cultural, intellectual, and commercial life involving flourishing Muslim, Christian, and Jewish cultures side by side. Muslim Spain was the great transmission belt of otherwise lost classical Greek literature and philosophy that had been translated into Arabic, preserved and passed on to Europe from Spain via translations from Arabic into Latin. Trade from China and Iran stretched across the Mediterranean, linking East Asian with Arab and Spanish culture, and on into Europe. For a period the Mediterranean was a largely uncontested Muslim sea. As the Spanish *reconquista* gradually extended its reach deeper into Spain over several hundred years, Muslim power finally collapsed in 1492. The last Muslims were expelled from Spain in 1609.[3]

Memory of the fall of Spain is still a living feature of Arab culture. Sophisticated Muslim refugees from Andalusia played prominent roles in the subsequent cultural development of the North African states. For the last 200 years before their final expulsion from Spain, increasing numbers of Spanish Muslims underwent another major new experience: Large Muslim societies were now forced to live under Christian rule, reversing many more hundred years of Christians living under Muslim rule. For upwards of a century the coexistence was comfortable; by 1601 Spanish Muslims were presented with the choice of conversion to Christianity, departure from Spain, or death. The notable religious tolerance toward Christians and Jews under Muslim rule in Spain had given way to the uncompromising zealotry of the Spanish Inquisition—that in many ways was a genuine Christian *jihad*. Jews and Muslims thus fled Spain, with large numbers of Jews emigrating to the Ottoman Empire, which was also known for its tolerance to Jews.

But Muslims living under Christian—or any non-Muslim—rule face special theological problems that go beyond mere potential discrimination. It is the religious mission of Muslims to establish Muslim governance wherever possible so that Muslims can live within an Islamic political, social, and cultural order in fulfillment of God's word. To live under non-Muslim rule is in effect to fail to create, or to be unable to create, a Muslim polity and political order, thereby diminishing the depth of Muslim life. Theoretically, then, for Muslims to live under non-Muslim rule presents theological hardships requiring special forbearance.

Muslims suddenly deprived of living under Muslim rule, therefore, suffer from what may be described as the "Andalusian syndrome, the fear of

extinction produced by the fate of the [Spanish] Moors, which would perma-
nently haunt Muslim society."[4] Rachid Ghannouchi, the leader in exile of the
Islamist Tunisian Renaissance Organization (al-Nahda), writes that

> the tragedy of the Muslims in Spain constitutes a model for the rigid
> Christian mentality during the Middle Ages when a population of no less
> than four million was annihilated at the hands of their Christian fellow cit-
> izens who [themselves] had lived in security under [Muslim] reign for
> many centuries. What is happening in Bosnia today at the hands of the
> Serbs is only a miniature of what happened in Andalusia.[5]

A similar fate met the Muslims of Hyderabad in India, who also maintained a high Muslim civilization as a minority, ruling for over 200 years over
an independent state with a majority Hindu population. The state was wiped
out upon independence in 1948, the Islamic culture disappeared, and the
Muslim ruling class was unseated and forced to accept lowly status or to flee
to Pakistan.[6]

These hardships are hardly unique in world history; many nations and
peoples have suffered sharp reversals, travail, and even disappearance. But
for Muslims, for whom history is the manifestation of the working out of
God's universal design and who are inclined to think in terms of an inter-
linked international Muslim community, the loss of these portions of community is perhaps felt more intensely—perhaps even as a "failure" of history.

"Umma," or Sense of Community

The Prophet Muhammad wrought not only a religious, but a social and
political revolution with the establishment of Islam. Coming into being in the
Arabian peninsula, where tribal loyalties commanded the ultimate political
commitment, Muhammad preached the creation and existence of a new
Islamic *umma,* or community that was to transcend all tribal, regional, and
ethnic differences in the formation of a new entity. All the world was open to
membership in Islam. Muslim prayer could be conducted upon any spot anywhere indoors or outdoors, as long as it was oriented toward Mecca.

> The prophet Muhammad is the only prophet who identified the whole
> earth as a mosque . . . . Islam is, among other things, a set of psychological
> devices about self-empowerment and making oneself at home everywhere
> around the globe, in unfamiliar as well as familiar surroundings, without
> having to know the language or the culture. Its prodigious world expan-

sion in the seventh century would not be understandable without taking into account its spatial component.[7]

The sense of community abides to this day as a strong feature of the psychology of Islam, in which grievances from one region can affect the attitudes of Muslims elsewhere. To whatever extent Christianity possessed an international sense of community, that impulse had almost completely disappeared at the popular level in the West by the twentieth century, except as a political pretext of state policy. Few organizations if any think of Christianity today as a *political* community. The one notable exception may be the Eastern Orthodox Church, which for historical reasons established various national branches such as Greek, Armenian, and Serbian, where to this day sense of religious community has been a powerful factor in survival in confronting other— even other Christian—communities.[8] In the modern period nationalism would seem to have considerably supplanted religion as a politically emotive force in most of the world. But operating in its capacity as a political community, Islam still functions as a politically emotive force, resembling nationalism in function.

The Shrinking of Islamic Empire

Muslim displacement from the Holy Land and the Levantine coast during the Crusades was only a temporary phenomenon, lasting about a century. Sicily, too, eventually reversed a long period of Muslim occupation and rule. Defeat and exile from Spain was permanent, however. The principal arena of the ongoing political and military confrontation of Islam and the Christian world continued with the rivalry between the Ottoman Turkish Empire and the Western states. This included Ottoman confrontation in the Mediterranean with re-Christianized Spain, with Venice, Genoa, France, and England. The Ottoman Turkish Empire, which spanned the twelfth to the twentieth century, stretched at various stages virtually from Gibraltar to the Balkans and up to the gates of Vienna, from Yemen in the Red Sea, and along the North African coast as well as portions of the Persian Gulf, constituting the last and greatest of the Muslim empires. Yet this empire, too, gradually faced a process of weakening and rollback, mostly at the hands of European powers, including Russia, Austria, and their small client states. One by one parts of the Balkans achieved independence from Istanbul: Hungary, Serbia, Romania, Greece, Albania, Bulgaria, and smaller princedoms—all of them

Christian except Albania, parts of Bosnia, and scattered Muslim enclaves.

Yet it would be a mistake to assume, as many commonly do today, that this span of nearly a millennium was one of unmitigated Muslim-Christian conflict and rivalry. The Ottoman Empire was part of the European state system. France joined with it against the Hapsburgs at one point. Other European states such as England supported it against the encroachments of Russia. The Ottomans themselves drew heavily upon the Christian community in the Balkans for governors and provincial officials; indeed, the empire's crack troops were drawn from a Christian levee that then converted to Islam to form these elite forces. Christians and Muslims were very well acquainted with each other and lived often side by side in many communities, each governed by its own religious and community laws operating autonomously. The Ottoman state was a multireligious state in which each religious community had its own rights and ruling structure; although subordinate to Muslims in political status, they were not in a state of war or specifically oppressed—unlike the Muslim experience in Spain after the reconquest. "The sick man of Europe," as the Ottoman Empire was called in the nineteenth century, was most definitely considered to be "of Europe" in a geopolitical sense.

The Era of Imperialism

Along with the collapse of the Ottoman Empire as the last great bastion of Muslim power, the Muslim world as a whole gradually fell under the imperial domination of Europe itself—the ultimate reversal of the medieval power equation. Nearly every portion of the Islamic world, from Indonesia to Gibraltar, up into Central Asia, and down into sub-Saharan Africa, at some period became the colonial possession of a host of European powers: England, France, Holland, Spain, Portugal, Italy, and Russia. Only Saudi Arabia and Afghanistan managed to remain independent.[9] Virtually all Muslims, therefore, remain intensely sensitive to questions of colonialism, particularly since colonialism sprang from nearby and familiar European neighbors, as the world system of power moved into the dramatic new phase of the imperial age. Christian domination over many aspects of life had theological implications for Muslims as well that made the occupation psychologically onerous.

Ali Mazrui summarizes some of the distortions that colonialism imposed on the Third World: "(1) urbanization without industrialization, (2) verbal education without productive training, (3) secularization without scientification (decline of religion without the rise of science), and (4) capitalist greed without capitalist discipline."[10] But other scars were also left, particularly in the important area of cultural damage.

In some cases, such as French control of Syria or British control of Jordan and Iraq, the mandate lasted only a few decades from the end of World War I. In the case of Algeria the colonial period under direct French rule lasted 132 years, with massive impact upon society as the state was completely incorporated into France. India's Muslims and Hindus were ruled by the British for hundreds of years. Russian rule over different parts of Muslim Central Asia varied from about 150 years to 300 years, coming to an end only "yesterday," in 1991.

The process of increasing control is described by François Burgat in the North African context that typifies most of the experience:

> The Western presence was preceded...by an earlier economic penetration that was itself the consequence of a growing financial dependence. It was in the transition to the military phase that this penetration took on the dimension of domination. . . . [such as] economic domination...appropriation of lands in simple commercial control . . . agricultural fields (increasingly devoted to export crops) and of roads, ports, and railways implanted to facilitate the draining of mineral and agricultural riches. . . .
>
> But beyond a certain threshold, economic domination meant social destruction. When the dominant economic logic of a society is disturbed, the social balance is also affected. . . . The net effect is the destruction of the social substratum of an entire system of production.
>
> It was only when the economic and social structures were profoundly damaged and the group's capacity to resist seriously weakened that foreign penetration gradually took over the cultural sphere and extended its ability to dominate completely.[11]

A Tunisian Muslim describes another facet of the experience:

> [Colonialism] begins what one may call the era of dualism. Dualism in the economy between the traditional sectors and modern sectors; dualism in the demographic distribution split between French colonists and indigenous populations; dualism of the State with the two-headed structure of the palace of the Bey and the Residence Generale; dualism of urban spaces with the contrast between the medina and the European-style city; dualism of the military; dualism of the administration, justice, education, religion, press, artistic and sports activities, etc.[12]

This process particularly affected the further development and modernization of Islamic thinking and of traditional cultural trends. In the account of an Algerian minister (Ben Aissa):

> Here in Algeria, it has produced a true cultural distress. After colonialism, we were submitted to a veritable ideological rape. For twenty years, the regime obscured Islam. For twenty years there was no higher Islamic education. In all the Western universities there were certificates, degrees, doctorates in Islamic theology. But in independent Algeria, there was not one institution of Islamic teaching. And when one was created, it was an institution for police. With us, the artisans of thought were Marxists. This was not a de-Islamicized generation . . ., it was a generation that never had been Islamicized, who had never learned anything. In Algeria, there were even people incapable of correctly pronouncing the word, "Koran." When they opened their mouths on Islam it was to say stupidities. They were alienated. Very good French intellectuals, no doubt . . . but they were not made for the Algerian people.[13]

The colonial period was therefore experienced as a period not only of foreign dominance but also of cultural humiliation and distortion. Its results are seen as still abiding in all the colonial world, but particularly in Muslim countries where traditional Muslim society was sharply displaced. A new Europeanized elite emerged that despite its strong nationalist impulses was often culturally alienated from its past and proceeded to impose its own elitist, quasi-Europeanized culture upon its own people. In effect these societies and cultures were deprived of the opportunity to develop naturally, organically; they were, rather, forced into a new mold in ways that did instant violence to the old orders; denied opportunity to gradually adapt on their own, they were, rather, pushed by foreigners into instant cultural revolution. This process created social and cultural bifurcation, a loss of the cultural tradition at the top of the political order that continues to extract a social cost even today. Thus the old quasi-Europeanized elite is now often charged with the creation of a corrupt or failing political order: the ruling National Liberation Front (FLN) in Algeria, the long rule of Bourgiba in Tunisia, the failed Nasserist revolution in Egypt, the Ba'th of Iraq, or the Shah of Iran. The Islamists today accuse these regimes not only of failure but of lack of authenticity, a distancing from the true social and cultural order of the nation that the Islamists now seek to resuscitate.

As simple a matter as the concept of time can even extract social anguish and evoke cultural clash. The early Muslim community established its own calendar at the time of the founding of the first Islamic state (as have Jews and Christians). Today, Western time and the Christian calendar have been imposed upon Muslim societies, as described by a Moroccan sociologist:

> We exist only in time defined by the West. We are exiles in Western time. The most horrible colonization is that which installs itself in your time, for there the wounds are to your dignity. Our tragedy is that our calendar more and more just defines our religious rituals and holidays. . . . [But] the mass of society, the millions of people who have never had access to modernity, who have been informally relegated to jobs where neither the minimum wage nor social benefits are guaranteed, ignore the official calendar and stick to the sacred calendar. . . . One of the manifestations of the class struggle in Morocco is the choice of calendar.[14]

Analytic objections can of course be raised against much of this line of reasoning by the Western observer. All technical and social change brings dislocations, even as it did in Western Europe at the time. Second, there is no guarantee that the "authentic" local order can function more effectively to solve deep-seated problems of state and society either. But there is a critical difference in perception when massive social and cultural change is imposed from outside by an alien culture and force, and when authoritarian elites associated with the former colonial power (at least in terms of education and culture) are perceived as the source of failed postcolonial government. Class overtones are also inevitably drawn in. Perceptions matter mightily in politics, and Islamists are drawing on these roots of social and cultural discontent. Cultural "wars" cut as deep as any other form of social confrontation.

The Export of Western Values

Muslim intellectuals, especially those who have incorporated large elements of Western thought into their own thinking, are often resentful at how they feel themselves victimized vis-à-vis their own peoples and coreligionists in their espousal of Western values. A North African intellectual explained it in the following terms:

> You, the West, have instructed us in the values of self-determination of nations after World War I with the Versailles Conference and the League of Nations. Yet it was precisely in that period that the Western states

proceeded to intensify their colonial hold over Muslim and other societies in the Third World. After World War II—a conflict that produced a level of killing among European states on a scale never seen in the Third World— the world was invited to join the United Nations and to sign the Universal Declaration of Human Rights. Yet again these rights were promptly ignored by most European states who were slow to grant the same rights to Third World peoples, who only grudgingly let go of colonies in the Arab world, after killing perhaps a million Algerians in the process, for example.

Algeria was not liberated until 1962, fourteen years after the signing of the Universal Declaration. Portuguese colonies were not liberated until thirty years after the Declaration in the late 1970s, the Muslim states of Central Asia were not liberated until 1991, and the peoples of South Africa have yet to be liberated.

So how can we square these realities with Western protestations about "universal values"? You tried to involve us in a white Western struggle against a white Soviet enemy. And finally, those of us in the Muslim World who have systematically stood for Western-derived values are now under the heaviest assault of all in our own societies—especially from the funda-mentalists—precisely because we have espoused and become identified with your "values." Our position as spokesmen for Westernization/mod-ernization has become all but untenable. You have destroyed us.[15]

Today Muslims are again confronted with yet a new Western campaign, this time about universal values and human rights, political liberalization, and the building of civil societies. Many Muslims are understandably cynical about this process to which they bring a certain sense of déjà vu. In their eyes the West sought to impose its values in the eighteenth century by talking about the spread of Christianity, and in the nineteenth century by talking about the *mission civilisatrice* and the "white man's burden." Today many Muslims see human rights, democratization, and the International Monetary Fund (IMF) as the latest devices by which the West seeks to impose its order on the Muslim and Third World, again in the name of universal values—read Western interests.

The Loss of Leadership of the Islamic World

Most Muslims are highly ambivalent about Mustafa Kemal Ataturk, the savior and founder of the modern Turkish state, who set Turkey on a prescribed course of Westernization. True, Ataturk initiated what was one of the Third World's most successful "national liberation movements" in the early 1920s, but it was a movement that explicitly rejected the Muslim past and most Muslim values. Above all, he destroyed the Caliphate, the spiritual head of the Sunni Islamic world. Ever since that date there has been no recognized head of the Sunni world. This fact has been a crippling one to the authority and evolution of Islam, akin to destroying the papacy for the Roman Catholic Church. Thus, although this act was not carried out by Western power, many Islamists interpret it as an act of Westernization—done to Western applause—and to the direct detriment of Islam. The goal is understood by many Muslim observers as having been to weaken the overall institution of Islam and its cultural heritage.

The nearest equivalent to head of Sunni Islam is perhaps the leadership of the Islamic University of al-Azhar in Cairo, a central place of Sunni jurisprudence and learning. Al-Azhar often issues *fatwas* (religious rulings) on issues of importance in modern Islam. Even though these pronouncements are primarily for Egypt itself, they have weight outside Egypt as well. Yet most Islamists view al-Azhar as a prisoner of the Egyptian regime, docilely delivering up rulings to support the current regime's policies. Al-Azhar's views and rulings thus carry only limited weight among the populace when al-Azhar is accused by the Islamists of lacking true theological independence and legitimacy.

Thus the Sunni Muslim world continues to lack formal leadership—a fact of some concern to clergy and religious leaders, and a factor that tends to weaken Islamic unity. If al-Azhar or some similar institution or figure did come to gain formal leadership of Sunni Islam, such a person or institution would quickly come into conflict with state authority; the state would make major efforts to subordinate it to its will. Islamists, therefore, would themselves not likely welcome the reestablishment of supreme Sunni power, since it would likely prove to be a conservative instrument of some state which would be used against Islamic radicalism. If an Islamist state could capture or recreate central Sunni leadership, it could be a powerful instrument of the Sunni radical movement, a force now largely absent except for diverse charismatic clerical figures in various states.

The Establishment of Israel

Although the establishment of Israel has by now been all but accepted by virtually all Muslim states as a *fait accompli*, the issue is not perceived in the

Muslim world as simply two parties quarreling over the same turf. Israel is seen very much in the context of the Crusader states, imposed in exactly the same area, established again by Western citizens and Western powers, and imposed upon the Muslim world. Nor is it viewed as akin, strictly speaking, to Western colonialism, whose period may run its course, at which time the colonialists go home. The establishment of Israel is seen as one of only two cases in modern history where Westerners have gone to a Third World state and established a permanent lasting foothold amidst another civilization and culture that has then been displaced.[16] South Africa is the other case; and even there long-term white dominance is now almost a thing of the past.

Whereas colonialism goes away eventually, so goes the rationale, Israel is a permanent Western outpost in the heart of the Muslim world. The state owes its existence to the West because it was Western persecution of European Jews that created the ideology of Zionism, and it was the European holocaust, committed against Jews by Europeans, that was the proximate cause for Jewish flight to Arab lands and the final foundation of the Jewish state. Since that time the new Jewish state has been directly and consistently supported by the West, including massive provision of funds and arms. Its existence has now become an irreversible fact. Muslims also point out that Muslims had historically lived basically at peace with Jews during most of Islamic history, and indeed it was the Ottoman Empire that accepted the Spanish Jews when they were expelled from Spain after 1492. The de facto expansion of Israel over time into the West Bank and southern Lebanon awakened fears of latent Israeli expansionism in the region, especially when most UN resolutions condemning it are perceived as having been functionally ignored by the West.

In the view of many Muslims the grievance is compounded by the series of Arab-Israeli wars that invariably demonstrated Israeli military superiority, through the use of Western arms, technology, and military doctrine, that imposed humiliating defeats upon the Arabs. The permanent Israeli military superiority over its Arab neighbors has been seen as an explicitly articulated policy goal of the United States under all U.S. administrations, regardless of events or Israel's policies. The issue of Israel, therefore, apart from its territorial and refugee aspects, carries a great deal of historical and emotional baggage that extends well beyond the immediate region and across the Muslim world, where it is still perceived as one of the great Muslim grievances against the West.

Western Intervention

Against the backdrop of the long cultural rivalry and imperialist tradition, the continuing process of Western political and military intervention into the Middle East helps perpetuate the paranoia in the Muslim perception. The presence of oil has of course raised the political stakes in the region, particularly when direct control of the oil fields by Western companies until the last few decades was considered the only acceptable norm and later, when at least Western ownership and control of the local oil companies was also viewed as nonnegotiable. It was this kind of thinking that in 1953 led the British intelligence service, supported by the Americans, to engineer the overthrow of Iran's Prime Minister Mossadegh in favor of restoring the power of the Shah of Iran—perhaps one of the most fateful and ill-conceived modern Western political interventions of all, in view of its long-term consequences in Iran.

Other acts of intervention have also left psychic wounds as well, of which the most prominent include the following:

- In 1956 Britain, France, and Israel invaded Egypt as a result of Nasser's nationalization of the Suez Canal.
- In 1958 the United States sent marines into Lebanon to protect the stability of that pro-Western state against the pan-Arab campaign against it, stemming primarily from Egypt.
- In 1967 in the Six-Day War between the Arab states and Israel the United States provided immediate intelligence support and military resupply to Israel in the course of the conflict.
- In 1973 the United States provided similarly extensive military and intelligence support to Israel during the Yom Kippur War.
- In 1974 the United States was active in providing covert support to the Iraqi Kurds against the regime of Saddam Hussein when Saddam was pursuing a policy of close relations with the Soviet Union and active hostility against the Shah.
- In 1982 the United States sent marines into Lebanon to oppose Syrian forces there after Israel's invasion and march to Beirut designed to wipe out the Palestine Liberation Organization (PLO).
- In 1985 the United States carried out extensive airstrikes against Libyan targets in Tripoli in response to a Libyan terrorist bombing in Germany.
- In 1986 the United States undertook a reflagging operation during the Iran-Iraq War to provide cover for Kuwaiti oil shipping in and out of the Gulf, an operation that involved numerous armed clashes with Iran,

including the accidental shooting down of an Iranian civilian airliner.

- In 1990–91 the United States gathered massive troop strength in Saudi Arabia and undertook the war against Iraq to liberate Kuwait, crushing the Iraqi military and subjecting the Iraqi people to a punishing embargo.

- In 1992–93 United States forces intervened in Somalia at the head of an overall UN force in what was initially a humanitarian mission but later became a broader military struggle against selected political leaders within Somalia—in a civil war for which many Somalis saw the United States as partially responsible because in earlier years it supported the military dictator Siad Barre.

- In 1993 the United States was still conducting periodic air and missile strikes against Iraq in which civilian loss of life occurred, and was active in supporting exile Iraqi opposition groups.

In addition to intervening militarily, the West, especially Washington, has actively supported selected Middle East regimes in the broader context of inter-Arab politics: Lebanon and Jordan against Nasser's Egypt; the Shah's Iran against Iraq; Kuwait against Iraq; Saudi Arabia against Nasser's Egypt and Saddam's Iraq; North Yemen against communist South Yemen; Egypt against Libya; Morocco against Algeria; and of course Israel against all regional states. This kind of support was often important in keeping friendly regimes in place. As a result, the United States is perceived to be an intrusive and active player in inter-Arab politics on both the overt and the covert level.

The preceding list is not meant to suggest that all Muslims opposed all these acts of U.S. policy. Nor is the list meant to be a balanced and objective picture of all aspects surrounding the intervention. It merely suggests the Muslim image of the frequency and scope of Western military and political intervention—leaving aside Israeli actions over the same period. However justified many of these policies appear to Western observers, it is imperative to recognize their impact on the Muslim world. They help create a broad paranoia, a sense that the peoples of the region are not masters of their own fate, especially when U.S. power is used to oppose those states and leaders who advocate pan-Arab policies, who seek to strengthen Arab unity and Arab military power. The Middle East is locally perceived as the one region of the world still languishing under tight neo-imperial control. Even Muslims who are basically sympathetic to many aspects of Western life and culture can suddenly react with anger when yet another incident of Western intervention convinces them that there are no limits to Western willingness to impose their strategic goals. This situation is the stuff of current and future paranoia, with some basis in reality. If Middle Easterners often display "plot mentalities," it is because they have, in fact, long been the victim of external "plots."

Islamic Weakness

Today Muslims see themselves as on the run all over the world. From the Hyderabad experience in India, to the displaced Palestinians, to Bosnia, Somalia, Central Asia, to oppression of Muslims in Kashmir and within India itself—all is seen of a piece. In a world of sharply disparate power relationships between North and South, Muslims believe they are under siege, caricatured, or persecuted as "enemies" with terrorist images. In Muslim eyes, Islamic culture through the actions of a tiny fanatic minority has now become equated with terrorism, leading to discrimination in the West, humiliating treatment at international airports, suspicion in the eyes of Americans and Europeans, and even religious slurs—the last ethnoreligious group which can still be ridiculed and caricatured with impunity in Western societies.

In the language of Western international media, terror is perceived to be directed at the West from Islam. Yet in a different sense, citizens of the Muslim world actually see themselves on the receiving end of "Western terror," seldom through the actions of individual terrorists, but through the far more powerful instrumentality of overwhelming Western military strength employed "tactically," but regularly, against the region. Many more Muslims have died at Western hands over the past century than Westerners have ever died at Muslim hands. As a result, many Muslims are inclined to draw broader conclusions: Most Muslims are convinced that Western policies are consciously dedicated to weakening Muslim power wherever it arises. The paranoia that flows from this historical experience strengthens the perception among even educated and thoughtful Muslims that the same old war against Islam is still carried on unchecked from 1,000 years ago, even though the means and methods have changed and are now more subtle. Why, they ask, did the West take such delight in Salman Rushdie's *Satanic Verses* and trumpet the book as a leading international *cause célèbre?* (Never mind that it was Khomeini who put it on the map.) The West is seen as invariably driven to put down every Muslim challenger, whether Nasser, Qadhafi, Khomeini, or Saddam Hussein, even if the power that they wield appears inconsequential in comparison with that of the West. The West is seen to be comfortable only with a supine Muslim world.

Given this vantage point, it is not surprising that when dictators such as Saddam Hussein do rise to challenge the West, the first instinct on the part of Muslim masses is in fact to applaud the challenger—precisely for standing up to the West, regardless of his other failings or goals. Weakness and a sense of oppression create a powerful (and perhaps indiscriminate) quest for dignity and equality.

The Dilemma of Modernization

In the face of the perceived onslaught of the West in all fields, Muslims are in effect left struggling to preserve their own boundaries—in all senses of the word.[17] First, boundaries relate to the very state boundaries of all Muslim states that have been drawn mainly by colonial powers. Today's physical boundaries of state borders and sovereign air space must be protected from external violation by Western power. Then there are the less tangible boundary problems: the imposition of new human rights values, new economic orders dominated by the West, the struggle to preserve Muslim cultural autonomy in the face of overwhelming and omnipresent Western media,[18] technological boundaries that possess their own urgency if one is to survive and compete in the modern world. Even behavioral boundaries are under siege: The new international acceptability of current Western sexual mores, and the revolutionary implications of the changing role of women in society—volatile even in the West in their overall social impact.

In the end the confrontation is in part about the dilemma of modernization. Few in the Muslim world would in principle eschew the imperative of modernization. But does modernization mean Westernization? How can the cultural and moral foundations of Islamic culture remain intact when acceptance of the material aspects of the West ultimately demands importation of the very philosophical bases of the culture that produced those material accomplishments? Does modernization imply full cultural submission to the West? Does it require submission to the absence of formal moral foundations that in the views of many Muslims and many Asians typify the perceived decay of the Western public order in crime, drugs, violence, the deterioration of the family, and absence of public values? Is it possible to take what is the best of the West in modernization and leave the worst? How does a culture preserve its identity—that most precious cultural anchor of any community? (One observer notes that the formality and rigid structure of Islam may provide the necessary glue to keep most Islamic societies intact in an era when

Third World states as a whole may be subjected to severe buffeting from a rising wave of anarchy, state collapse, and social chaos.[19]) This dilemma is faced by Muslims today in looking at the West and the onslaught of modernization. It is Islam that appears to offer a more deeply rooted cultural anchor than modern secular nationalism.[20]

Notes

1. See Albert Hourani, *Islam in European Thought* (Cambridge: Cambridge University Press, 1991), p. 10.

2. Ali A. Mazrui, *Cultural Forces in World Politics* (Portsmouth, New Hampshire, UK: Heinemann, 1990), p. 30.

3. Ira M. Lapidus, *A History of Islamic States* (New York: Cambridge University Press, 1988), pp. 378–392.

4. Akbar S. Ahmed, *Discovering Islam: Making Sense of Muslim History and Society,* (London: Routledge, 1988), p. 2.

5. Rachid Ghannouchi, "Islam and the West: Realities and Prospects." *Inquiry,* March-April 1993, p. 47.

6. Ahmed, *Discovering Islam,* pp. 160–171.

7. Fatima Mernissi, *Beyond the Veil* (Cambridge, MA: Schenkmann, 1975), p. x.

8. Hence the violent emotions between Serbs and Croats, who are ethnically identical and speak the same language but are Orthodox and Roman Catholic respectively.

9. The territory of modern Turkey, created out of the ruins of the Ottoman state, escaped with only brief, partial European military occupation for a few years after World War I and was never subject to colonialism. This fact has been one of the psychological strengths of the Turkish state and society today.

10. Mazrui, *Cultural Forces in World Politics,* pp. 5–6.

11. François Burgat, *The Islamic Movement in North Africa* (Austin: University of Texas, 1993), pp. 43–44.

12. Ibid., p. 45.

13. Quoted in ibid. p. 47.

14. Fatima Mernissi, *Islam and Democracy: Fear of the Modern World* (CA: Addison-Wesley, 1992), pp. 141–143.

15. Author's personal interview with a North African intellectual in government, April 1993.

16. This is the usual Muslim view. The land of Israel, of course, was not arbitrarily chosen by Western Jews as a place of refuge from European persecution; there were always Jews in Jerusalem, and the area had been the site of earlier Jewish states in ancient times. Nonetheless, Muslims are impressed with the European provenance of the Zionist concept, the European character of the Israeli elite, and Israel's close strategic orientation with the West.

17. Mernissi, *Beyond the Veil*, pp. xvii–xviii.

18. A concern shared by the French as much as by Muslims, for example.

19. See Robert Kaplan, "The Coming Anarchy." *Atlantic*, February 1994.

20. See the thesis of Mark Juergensmeyer in *The New Cold War?: Religious Nationalism Confronts the Secular State* (Los Angeles: University of California, 1993), in which he argues that the phenomenon of religious nationalism is affecting virtually *all* religions and states today.

4

CONTEMPORARY DILEMMAS POSED TO THE WEST BY THE ISLAMIC WORLD

An extraordinary variety of post–Cold War foreign and security policy challenges faced by the West have an Islamic dimension. This does not automatically suggest that Islam itself presents a unified challenge to the West. But the strength and diversity of Western concerns and the potential for these concerns to interact with Muslim perceptions suggest a future in which the Islamic factor is likely to become more prominent in international affairs generally and Western security in particular. From an analytic perspective, it is important to examine existing and emerging problems on their own merits, to separate key issues and explore their implications for the future strategic environment and Western policy. For these purposes, a broad and useful distinction can be made between hard security issues, such as proliferation and terrorism, and softer societal and security-related questions such as migration and human rights.

Islam, Democracy, and Human Rights

The revolutionary changes in the former Soviet Union and Eastern Europe and the acceleration of political change in Asia, Africa, and elsewhere have made the promotion of democracy as a stabilizing force in international affairs a core objective of Western policy makers. But the spread of democracy also poses dilemmas concerning both process and outcome in developing societies.[1] Nowhere are these dilemmas more apparent and more challenging than in the Greater Middle East (here understood to include North Africa and Central Asia), where Islamic political movements have emerged as the dominant opposition to established regimes. At the same time, and in the absence of Cold War imperatives, concern for human rights is becoming increasingly important in relations between the West and the Third World in general. On the European periphery the character of the European Community's relations with its Islamic neighbors, from Morocco to Turkey, has already been strongly affected by human rights issues. Moreover, questions of democracy, Islam, and human rights are closely linked.[2] The violent suppression of Islamic movements in North Africa, for example, draws Western criticism, while hard-pressed regimes insist that the United States and Europe view Islamic fundamentalism as a security issue rather than a human rights issue.

On both sides of the Atlantic the debate over whether Islam has emerged as a new ideological threat has acquired greater intensity in the wake of the Gulf War, with active discussion of the distinctions between "radical" and "moderate" or mainstream Islam and the external intentions of Islamic activists. The latter has been a particularly thorny issue, because the foreign policy aims of Islamic opposition movements are often obscure, poorly articulated, or articulated with a view to reassuring Western observers. In the case of Algeria's Islamic Salvation Front (FIS), for example, foreign and security policy issues are hardly mentioned. In Algeria, as elsewhere, the Islamic opposition speaks primarily of national reform and moral rectification. Very little has been said about relations with the West outside the standard condemnation of the corrosive effects of Western culture. Where Islamic leaders have been outspoken on external issues, principally in Iran and Sudan, the rhetoric has not been encouraging. In the view of one observer, Islamists "are, and are likely to remain, anti-Western, anti-American and anti-Israel."[3] In fact, these sentiments are hardly limited to Islamist quarters within Muslim societies. In Egypt, for example, the government's pro-Western policies contrast sharply with the widespread antipathy to the United States and Europe among a broad spectrum of intellectuals and the public.[4]

An alternative view admits that Islamic government, though not necessarily incompatible with democratic process, may well develop along undemocratic lines ("One man, one vote, one time"). But on the foreign policy front, Islamism does not automatically prevent active cooperation with the West. Saudi Arabia, a "fundamentalist" regime by many measures, provides a striking example. In this view, Islam is but one of many components in the foreign and security policy picture, and not necessarily the most important one, even in places such as Teheran. Questions of national interest and regional balance are just as likely to condition the behavior of Islamic regimes as any other. Moreover, if anti-Westernism is not a given, it follows that the internal as well as external policies of emerging Islamic regimes may be shaped by the policies taken toward them while in opposition.[5] Confluence with Western values and international objectives may not be automatic, but nor is it inconceivable. The interruption of the democratic process in Algeria has led to a situation in which radical elements within the FIS have come to the fore, making the prospects for longer-term democratization and "peaceful coexistence" with the West that much more remote.[6] Although there is a general awareness of this reality in Western debates about Islamism in Algeria and elsewhere, potentially sharp differences in view can be seen within the West. Whereas U.S. and southern European observers have been inclined to recognize the utility, even inevitability, of dialogue with "moderate" Islamists, French policy to date has been more wary.

The role of Iran and Sudan in furthering the spread of radical Islam is particularly significant in Western perception because it seems to lend a tangible, geopolitical character to what would otherwise be a more diffuse perception of risk.[7] The Egyptian, Algerian, Tunisian, and Turkish governments have been at the forefront in pointing to the role of external powers in fomenting Islamic opposition and attacks on secular institutions and in providing money, training, and weapons for insurgents. In some cases these assessments are broadly correct, and they have certainly had an effect on Western opinion. But it would be incorrect to assume that external factors are responsible for political instability and problems of internal security in such places as Egypt or Algeria. As virtually all analysts of the situation in these countries agree, the Islamic opposition, including its violent aspects, stems from long-standing crises of economic and political development. If Iranian and Sudanese involvement were entirely absent, it is most likely that conditions of instability in Cairo and Algiers would remain essentially unchanged. Nonetheless, the fact of Iranian and Sudanese involvement has allowed embattled regimes to make a stronger case for support in the West by emphasizing the security and geopolitical aspects of the Islamic challenge. The strongest proponents of "Islamic arc" and "domino" theories are to be found in Middle Eastern capitals rather than Western capitals.[8]

Developments in North Africa are likely to prove a watershed in terms of perceptions and policies on all sides. The abortive 1990 elections in Algeria, in which the FIS gathered roughly 70 percent of the popular vote, followed by a thinly masked military coup, set the stage for a progressive escalation of the conflict between government and Islamic opposition forces. The U.S. and European response has, in broad terms, been to express regret at the current situation and to await the resumption of the democratic process—an approach that has been interpreted by the Islamic opposition and some Western observers as providing tacit support for the Algerian junta. At base,

Western attitudes toward the Algerian situation reflect a marked pessimism about the outlook for democracy in an Islamic setting.[9] The remarkably open political discourse leading to the 1990 elections was widely applauded, but the results themselves produced evident unease, reinforced by comments from the FIS leadership that were at best ambivalent on the question of democracy in Algeria.

The spiraling violence and repression in Algeria and Egypt raise conflicting emotions among Western observers. Attacks by radical Islamists on prominent secular figures as well as foreigners and Copts are viewed with repugnance.[10] At the same time, the hard-line policies adopted in Algiers and Cairo are also seen as part of the problem, eliminating legitimate opposition, leaving the field to the most violent forces and permitting a general deterioration of human rights. The human rights problem, serious in its own right, also has implications for regional balances and Western strategy. If instability and human rights abuses make extensive security and security assistance relationships with Egypt (and perhaps elsewhere) untenable, broader initiatives predicated on these ties, including movement toward a comprehensive Arab-Israeli settlement, could be jeopardized. In fact, the pressure on relations caused by human rights issues is multidimensional. Hard-pressed regimes in the Muslim world are increasingly resistant to what they view as the imposition of Western values in a tenuous security situation. Western governments feel obliged to pursue human rights concerns with increased vigor in the post–Cold War environment. In doing so, they are also responding to the weight of public opinion, which views human rights objectives are seen as an integral part of foreign policy. The result has been a climate of growing strain between Western states and even "friendly" regimes in the Muslim world. At the same time, emphasis on human rights may be an increasingly important area of common ground between the Islamic opposition groups and the West. In places such as Egypt, Algeria, and Tunisia, Islamists have a pragmatic interest in the ability of Western pressure to make existing regimes adhere to minimum standards of conduct in their treatment of political opponents.

Migration and Social Cohesion

In many ways the central question of this study is not Islam *and* the West but Islam *in* the West. Migration into Europe from Islamic countries around the Mediterranean and further afield has emerged as a leading issue at public and official levels. At first glance the role of religion would appear to be a peripheral one. The phenomenon of large-scale migration from all quarters, from East to West as well as from South to North, and its social consequences looms large in current political debates. On closer examination however, cultural and religious concerns are never far from the surface of discussion about migration in the West. The evolution of attitudes and policy in this area will play a key role in shaping relations with the Muslim world in light of the dramatic disparity in demographic trends between North and South on the European periphery.[11] A second and related disparity in economic performance and labor requirements between North and South will serve as an additional engine for migration from Muslim countries to the West.[12]

The scale of migration from the Maghreb (primarily to France and southern Europe), from Turkey (primarily to Germany and Scandinavia), and from the Indian subcontinent (largely to Britain and North America) is substantial and has resulted in the establishment of large Muslim communities across Western Europe and, to a lesser but growing degree, in North America.[13] In countries such as France and Germany, where Maghrebi and Turkish workers have been a part of the economic and social scene for generations, post–Cold War political changes and growing unemployment have combined to produce an uncongenial and sometimes dangerous atmosphere for foreigners in general and Muslims in particular. The current pressure stems not only from right-wing violence but also from the movement toward zero-immigration policies on the part of mainstream parties and governments. With the progressive elimination of controls on the movement of people within the European Community, migration policy is also acquiring a strong multilateral character. Countries on the European periphery find themselves under pressure as the gateways for migration from the poor and increasingly populous South to the rich North. Moreover, Portugal, Spain, Italy, and Greece, all traditional net exporters of labor, now find themselves in the uncomfortable position of receiving ever larger numbers of economic migrants and refugees from Muslim countries. Spain and Italy, in particular, have served as conduits for migration to industrial centers elsewhere in Europe for some time. With growing affluence these countries have also become destinations in their own right, against a backdrop of recent right-wing and anti-immigrant electoral successes in both countries. Across the Atlantic, Islam is an increasingly visible presence, with some 6 million Muslims in the United States, but as yet there is relatively little sensitivity to Islam as a culture and a religion.

The cultural tension between national and migrant communities in Europe, often spilling over into overt racism, is heightened by the relatively religious and traditional nature of Muslim migrants, many of whom come from rural areas such as southeastern Turkey.[14] They are not easily assimilated into urban life in the West, and in many cases the sense of isolation and alienation experienced by refugees and migrants does not encourage closer integration. Indeed, under these circumstances ethnicity and religion take on additional significance. The roughly 1.5 million Turkish residents in Germany are, for the most part, more traditional and observant in their practice of Islam than their counterparts in Turkey; in fact, many affluent Turks feel that the rural, relatively religious guest workers in Germany present an "unfavorable," that is, a Middle Eastern, image of Turkey abroad. Muslim political activists, often constrained in their ability to organize at home, have also found an easier atmosphere in exile. This too has contributed to European (and, increasingly, U.S.)concern about "fundamentalist" activity on the part of political refugees.

Beyond cultural frictions and intolerance, the experience of the Gulf War also raised fears about the potential spillover effects of instability and intervention in the Muslim world on Muslim communities in the West. To date these fears have proven largely groundless. Pro-Saddam demonstrations in North Africa did not produce any significant politicization across the Mediterranean. The Kurdish case is far less clear. The Kurdish Workers Party (PKK) has reportedly been engaged in widespread extortion within the Turkish community in Germany, as well as drug-smuggling and other criminal activities aimed at financing the insurgency in southeastern Turkey.[15] The recent wave of PKK-led violence across Western Europe only reinforces the impression that Muslim migrants bring Middle Eastern turmoil to Europe. In their efforts to limit the political activities of potentially radical groups on their territory, European governments will likely worsen an already deteriorating climate for Muslim immigrants.

Muslim migration to Europe and the United States also has potentially serious implications for relations at the broader level of foreign and security policy. European unease at the prospect of potentially unrestricted migration and the difficulty of absorbing a country of 60 million Muslims (perhaps 90 million by the turn of the century) plays a strong if largely unspoken role in Europe's unwillingness to encourage Turkey's aspirations for membership in the European Union. The reinvigoration of the European Union's "Mediterranean policy," including extensive schemes for development assistance and investment along the southern littoral, is aimed largely at stemming the tide of migration. At the same time policy makers in Lisbon, Madrid, Paris, and Rome are sensitive to the importance of the migration "safety valve" in limiting social unrest and instability in the South, with all that this implies for security in a North-South context.[16] The deportation or extradition of Muslim activists resident in the United States would have clear significance for U.S. relations with Arab regimes and would pose the sort of dilemmas European governments have faced for many years.

Migration policy and the treatment of Muslim residents in Europe will play a substantial role in the overall character of relations between Islam and the West. Leaving aside the question of Western policy toward Bosnia, addressed in more detail below, violence against Muslim workers and their families in France, Germany, and to a much lesser extent Italy is front-page news in the Muslim world. The security of Turks abroad has become an important component of Turkey's expanding foreign policy and security debate and has emerged as a leading issue in bilateral relations with Germany. In North Africa the widespread perception that Islam is being portrayed as the new enemy in post–Cold War Europe affects elite as well as public attitudes in ways that could become evident in future crises. More positively, the strong incentives for a north-south bargain on migration policy could stimulate cooperation along political, economic, and military lines with positive implications for stability and relations between Muslim countries and the West.[17] Finally, developments within the Muslim world could present new migration dilemmas, especially for France and southern Europe. The advent of new Islamic regimes in Algeria or Egypt, or the deterioration of the climate facing secularists elsewhere, including Turkey and the countries of Central Asia, could produce an additional influx of middle-class refugees, Mediterranean "boat people" fleeing instability, intolerance, and declining economic opportunity.[18]

Nationalism and Ethnic Conflict

It is axiomatic that the end of the Cold War and the disintegration of the Soviet Union have released destabilizing forces of nationalism and ethnic friction both within Europe and on its periphery. Islam is at the very center of some of the most serious contemporary conflicts of this nature, from the Balkans to the Caucasus and Central Asia. Within the Muslim world itself conflict along ethnic lines is a feature of inter- and intrastate conflict in the Middle East, the Indian subcontinent, Asia, and North and sub-Saharan Africa. At the broadest level, the interaction of Islam and nationalism will be a leading aspect of Western concern for some time to come.

In many respects Islamism in the greater Middle East and assertive nationalism in the Balkans and Caucasus spring from similar roots. Both have been encouraged by the erosion of state legitimacy and economic privation. Both phenomena can be attributed in large measure to reaction against foreign domination: on the one hand to the colonial experience and its legacy; on the other, to the stifling control of the Warsaw Pact years.[19] At the same time, Islamism itself can be seen as a reaction to the disappointing progress of secular Arab nationalism.[20] Outside the Arab world Turkey's secular ideology, as embodied in the Ataturk legacy, occupies a special place in Islamist demonology.

Religious friction in the Balkans, in particular the confrontation between Islam and Orthodox Christianity, has been intimately connected with national aspirations and the evolution of the conflict in the former Yugoslavia. Should the conflict spread to become a wider Balkan war, it would do so largely along confessional lines, with largely Muslim Bosnia, Albania, and Turkey ranged against Orthodox Serbia, Greece, and potentially Russia.[21] Even short of such apocalyptic scenarios, the existence of some 9 million Muslims in the Balkans creates a responsibility for Turkey as a neighboring Muslim country. The situation in the former Yugoslavia has almost certainly strengthened the position of the religious and nationalist right wing in Turkish politics, contributing to the impressive showing by the Islamist Welfare Party in Turkey's 1994 municipal elections and providing the spark for violent anti-Western demonstrations in Ankara and Istanbul during the Gorazde confrontation.

Indeed, the plight of the Bosnian Muslims and the perceived inaction of the West have become a *cause célèbre* among Muslims of every political stripe, from secular Turkey to fundamentalist Iran. The Islamic Conference Organization (ICO) has been active in calling for an end to the arms embargo against Bosnia and intervention to stem Serbian aggression.[22] At least 500 volunteers from Saudi Arabia, Afghanistan, Iran, Pakistan, Turkey, and elsewhere in the Muslim world have reportedly joined the Muslim forces in Bosnia.[23] Iran has been the most assertive in calling for direct intervention, including the supply of heavy weapons; clandestine arms shipments from Islamic sources abroad are almost certainly arriving in Bosnia. The latter reportedly included several Stinger anti-aircraft missiles originally supplied by the United States to the Afghan resistance.[24] The Bosnian government itself has begun to call for greater assistance from Islamic states, including the formation of "international brigades," and Bosnian spokespersons have used thinly veiled references to potential Islamic intervention as a means of encouraging Western response.[25]

Material assistance to the Bosnian Muslims is largely symbolic. But the sense of Western reluctance to intervene on behalf of Muslims in the Balkans has encouraged a widespread belief throughout the Muslim world that the West is pursuing a deliberate strategy aimed at removing the last vestiges of Islam in Europe, a view reinforced by Serbian and Croatian comments.[26] At a minimum, Western policy is seen as a manifestation of racism and indifference. In this context Europeans are seen as the leading villains. U.S. failure to act is simply regarded with immense disappointment in moderate Muslim circles. Alternatively, it is interpreted as a demonstration of Washington's unwillingness to intervene on behalf of Muslims without oil, in contrast to the intervention in Kuwait.[27]

In the view of many observers in the Muslim world as well as the West, European and U.S. policy toward Bosnia has, along with the Gulf War, helped to fuel the rise of militant Islam in North Africa and elsewhere.[28] Just as the intervention against Iraq demonstrated the ability of events in the Gulf to affect North Africa and the security of Europe, so the conflict in the former Yugoslavia points to the ability of ethnic conflict and separatism in Europe to influence the stability of the greater Middle East. Nor is this likely to prove a transitory phenomenon. An outcome that does not permit the return of as many of 500,000 of Bosnia's 2 million Muslims displaced since the start of hostilities could well result in the creation of a Palestinian-type problem in Europe, with all that this might mean for political violence within Western societies.

It would be a mistake, however, to conclude as many Muslim observers have that Western opinion is unresponsive to the plight of the Bosnian Muslims. U.S. policy makers and others are extremely uncomfortable with the notion of a settlement that does not do justice to Muslim claims. In Europe, where a more calculated geopolitical approach to the conflict has prevailed in foreign and defense ministries, some leading intellectuals have adopted the Bosnian crisis as a *cause célèbre*. The most prominent example of this could be seen in France, where the philosopher Bernard-Henri Levy and others campaigned under the slogan "Europe begins in Sarajevo."[29]

Ethnic and separatist movements in the Caucasus, in Central Asia, and within Russia itself are commonly seen as evolving to a significant extent along Muslim-Christian lines, although the stakes of conflict are largely territorial.[30] The conflict between Armenia and Azerbaijan engages the sympathies and the danger of direct intervention of Turks and Russians. Instability flowing from ethnic tensions within and among the southern republics of the former Soviet Union has already inflamed Moscow's strategic sensitivities and raised the specter of Russian conflict with Islamic states on its periphery. To the extent that Islam continues to play a more prominent role in the political evolution of Central Asia, the interaction of religion and nationalism will acquire even greater significance. As these emerging states struggle to define their role between North and South, East and West, the strength of the Islamic factor will influence the character of Western as well as Russian options in dealing with this vast region.[31]

North-South Relations: To Have and Have Not

Relations between "North" and "South" in the post–Cold War World may be largely synonymous with relations between Islam and the West. At the very least, there will be a close connection between both sets of relationships in Western perception and policy. In the case of European relations across the Mediterranean, the convergence of North-South and Islam-West issues is most striking. Elsewhere, the overlap, though less complete, still holds. Islam has long been a prominent social and political force in the Third World, and some of the most active countries of the nonaligned movement have been Muslim, including Algeria, Indonesia, Malaysia, and Egypt (India, another leading member, has a substantial Muslim minority). In the absence of an active East-West competition, the notion of nonalignment in international affairs has lost much if not all of its meaning. But the institutional framework of non-alignment and the desire for international activism remain. After the Cold War the movement has begun to refashion itself to defend the interests of have-nots in a manner that presupposes a new political, economic, and strategic divide between north and south.[32]

On matters ranging from political development to human rights and intervention, the ICO has already become a leading forum for pursuing what once might have been characterized as a Third World or non-aligned agenda, with such unlikely actors as Saudi Arabia in the vanguard. The ICO as well as the nonaligned movement has debated policy toward Bosnia, with non-Muslim members of the nonaligned movement, many facing separatist challenges of their own, far less willing to censure Serbia or intervene on Bosnia's behalf. Within the ICO, calls for intervention have been commonplace. But concerns about precisely which countries might take the lead in arming Bosnia's Muslims have prevented consensus on action beyond humanitarian relief. Nonetheless, the requirements of diplomacy within the ICO can be expected to play an increasing role in the policies of countries such as Turkey not previously known for their Islamic concerns.

Another area of potential convergence between Islam and "southern" politics may well be the emerging identity of the largely Muslim states of Central Asia. The external policy orientation of these new states remains an open question. The resurgence of Islam as a political force in these areas, coupled with the inclination of Muslim as well as Western observers to categorize the new states of Central Asia as part of an expanded Middle East, will have important implications on all sides.[33] The sudden "discovery" of these vast Muslim regions will change the geopolitical balance within the Muslim world and perhaps the character of the discourse between Islam and the West, with new issues coming to the fore (Nagorno-Karabagh or Abkhazia in addition to Palestine?). Should the Islamic factor become dominant in the political evolution of the Caucasus and Central Asia, the triangular relationship among Russia, its Islamic periphery, and the West could also become a key dimension of the new strategic environment. Fear of Russia's Islamic neighbors has become a mainstay in the political imagery of right-wing Russian nationalists and is influencing the views of more moderate politicians and strategic analysts in Moscow. If the perception of an Islamic threat helps to reawaken a more assertive Russian policy, not only toward the "near-abroad" but in international affairs generally, the consequences for the West could be substantial. In some cases there may be a convergence of interests in dealing with events in the Muslim world. It is just as likely that the consequences will be negative: With Russian policy on the Muslim periphery cutting against Western interests, as in the proposed revision of the Conventional Forces in Europe (CFE) Treaty provisions, or moving in overtly provocative ways (e.g., intervention in the Balkans or the Caucasus). Indeed, a truly resurgent nationalist stance in Moscow could even lead to a broader revival of east-west political competition in the Muslim world, although Russian nationalists cannot be well placed to forge a cooperative relationship with the most potent opposition elements, the Islamists.

Leaving aside security issues, the broader north-south agenda after the Cold War will inevitably influence relations between Islam and the West, and frictions along have and have-not lines may interact with religious and cultural cleavages to worsen relations between the "rich" north and its largely poor and Muslim periphery.[34] Already thorny questions of "conditionality," or the linkage between human rights conditions or economic policy in recipient countries and the provision of economic assistance, would be further complicated by the advent of Islamic regimes in North Africa or Central Asia, although this might in the end be less disruptive of aid relationships than prolonged turmoil. The linkage between human rights and political reform with aid has been a significant factor in the European Community's relations with Morocco and Turkey. Sudan's human rights record and allegations of involvement in international terrorism have resulted in a cutoff of U.S. and much European economic assistance.

Environmental and resource issues, prominent on the global North-South agenda, will also be part of the fabric of relations between Islam and the West. Although the awareness of environmental security is more highly developed in the West—much of the Muslim world, like the Third World in general, places a higher priority on economic development and regards environmental policy as a luxury—interest elsewhere is growing, particularly in the wake of the Gulf War.[35] The transnational character of many environmental problems suggests that this will be a potentially promising area for cooperation along the Eurasian periphery, and this will necessarily mean cooperation across religious and developmental lines. A good deal has already been achieved through international efforts in the Mediterranean, where Israel has also been a significant player, and similar patterns of cooperation can be envisioned in the Black Sea, where environmental problems are acute.[36]

Both Europe and the United States will be important sources of development assistance and investment for the Greater Middle East, including North Africa and Central Asia. In many cases Western governments will view economic involvement in the Muslim world as a contribution to stability and as a way to reduce migration pressure. For this reason, among others, the European Union can be expected to play an overwhelmingly important role in the economic as well as political engagement of the Maghreb countries. This has already found expression in the "Five plus Five" process bringing together the members of the Arab Maghreb Union (AMU) and key European Mediterranean countries, namely, Portugal, Spain, France, Italy, and Malta. The European Union has also been engaged in a general attempt to revise its Mediterranean trade, investment, and aid policies, although the movement toward a unified European market raises serious questions about the future prospects for North African and Middle Eastern, not to mention Central Asian, access to European markets.

Already extensive energy ties between Europe and the Islamic periphery are set to expand as a new high-capacity pipeline is built to carry Algerian natural gas to the European market via Morocco and Spain. At the opposite end of the Mediterranean, the construction of new pipelines between Azerbaijan and Turkey will permit new energy exports through the

Mediterranean. These new links hold the potential for a greater degree of economic interdependence between North and South, Islam and the West. In an era when economic sanctions have become a feature of international affairs and, in the views of many Third World observers, a frequent prelude to military intervention, new energy ties will also mean new strategic variables and new points of vulnerability and interdependence in times of crisis. Ultimately, the security of these new economic links will turn not only on the specifics of bilateral relations such as those between Turkey and the Gulf states or between Libya and Italy but also on the character of relations between the Islamic world and the West.

European economic integration and the increasingly "European" character of the foreign and security policies of Spain, France, and Italy—traditionally important European interlocutors for Muslim countries—have already stimulated efforts at regional integration across the Muslim world. Examples include the AMU in North Africa and the Economic Cooperation Organization (ECO) bringing together Turkey, Iran, Pakistan, and the Muslim states of Central Asia. Leaving aside the very limited success of the AMU and the tentative character of the ECO, it is nonetheless clear that the progress of the European Union has raised interest in the integration option within the Muslim world. Perhaps more significantly, at the political as well as economic level there has been a desire for initiatives that might give individual Muslim countries greater diplomatic weight in dealing with Washington and, above all, Brussels.[37] One consequence of the growing salience of trade and assistance relations with the European Union may well be a problematic division of interests and perceptions among Europe, the United States, and the states of the Muslim periphery. In the absence of Cold War imperatives the incentives for U.S. engagement in the economic and political development of the Maghreb, and possibly the Caucasus and Central Asia as well, will be marginal. Although Europeans play a leading developmental role in these regions, the United States will continue to be a military power of potentially overwhelming consequence. This sharp division of interests and instruments may make a concerted Western approach to regional issues on Europe's Muslim periphery more difficult to sustain. It may also reinforce the belief, prevalent across the Muslim world, that the United States is less interested in the long-term political and economic development of the Middle East than in encouraging a predictable security environment.

The conviction that economic underdevelopment encourages the rise of Islamic radicalism is widely shared in the West. The tremendous gap between demographic trends and economic growth in North Africa and elsewhere encourages this conclusion, and few analysts disagree about the long-term interaction of economic and political factors in developing countries. Yet the likelihood that Western assistance and investment will forestall political revolutions already underway is probably less than governments hope. Increasing constraints on legal migration will only increase the pressure on hard-pressed regimes. Given the competing claims on limited economic development funds emanating from Eastern Europe, Russia, and the southern portions of the European Union itself, as well as financial stringency in the United States, the prospects for Western assistance and investment on a scale sufficient to reverse destabilizing trends within a politically relevant period are slim. The challenge of political Islam in places such as Algeria and Egypt is immediate; the prospects for significant economic improvement are distant.[38]

In looking beyond these issues, it is worth repeating that post–Cold War relations between the Muslim world and the West will interact with, and in many cases be subsumed by, broader questions of North-South relations. At the same time, the search for new ideological bases within the Third World as traditional notions of nonalignment, socialism, and anticolonialism lose their relevance may increase the attractiveness of political Islam as a dimension of external as well as internal policy in the South. Western observers will continue to have cause for anxiety about the political and economic crises emanating from the Muslim world and the consequences for the international system, regional stability, and Western societies themselves. These dilemmas may be most acute on the European periphery, but the effects will be felt more broadly and could include new strains within the West with regard to policy toward the Muslim world. Moving from political and economic issues to discussion of security issues per se, the Western sense of the centrality of the Islamic factor is even more pronounced.

Islamic Instability as a Threat to World Order

As one Western commentator has observed, "The Gulf War was a spectacular example of Northern military force being deployed in the South, and it is unlikely to be the last."[39] Despite the largely symbolic participation of Muslim countries in the Gulf coalition, one could just as well interpret the conflict as a striking example of Western intervention in the Muslim world—and this is precisely the interpretation that many popular and elite observers in the Middle East prefer. How tensions within Western societies over immigration and the integration of Muslim communities are resolved will also have more direct security consequences. According to one pessimistic assessment, if these tensions are not resolved peacefully, "Europe will risk creating new divisions and conflicts, such as a white, wealthy and Christian 'Fortress Europe' pitted against a largely poor, Islamic world. That could lead to terrorism and another forty years of small, hot wars."[40] Looking ahead, to what extent will the "Islamic factor" make itself felt in security terms? To what extent is Islam already a significant element in Western strategic perceptions, and what are the central issues?

Western policy makers and publics tend to view the Muslim world, especially the Middle East, as a place where political violence is endemic and inter- and intrastate conflicts are commonplace. Moreover, as the earlier discussion of historical images suggests, the West has been prone to thinking of Islam itself as a "peculiarly violent and aggressive faith," a particularly unfortunate legacy, since Islam remains the dominant faith along Europe's entire periphery.[41] Contemporary experience of conflict between Israel and its Arab neighbors, the Iranian revolution, war between Iraq and Iran, the invasion of Kuwait, civil war in Lebanon, violence involving the Kurdish populations of Iraq, Iran, and Turkey, and conflict in Western Sahara (and this is hardly an exhaustive list) have reinforced the perceived linkage of Islam with violent political change and war. Moreover, in the absence of Cold War, superpowerimposed constraints, the potential for conflict involving leading regional states may be increasing. Thus it is argued that under Cold War conditions Moscow would never have "allowed" Saddam Hussein to invade Kuwait for fear of the escalatory risks. From the Western perspective as well, Cold War realities dictated a healthy measure of concern about the escalatory dangers of regional conflict in the Middle East, dangers evident as early as 1956 with the Soviet nuclear threats over the Suez Canal.

Many Western observers express a nostalgic longing for the old East-West competition—dangerous but predictable, especially as regards the behavior of client states. The end of the Cold War has brought with it a sense that ambitious actors in the Islamic world such as Iran, Iraq, Syria, and Libya are now free to pursue more aggressive regional policies. In reality the freedom of action available to these countries is likely to be greatly constrained by the absence of Soviet patronage and the overwhelming significance of Western, above all U.S. power and influence. In either case the pressures on Western policy arising from the seemingly endless tensions and conflicts in the Muslim world are great and will contribute to a continuing diplomatic burden and a diffuse sense of siege. As Western policy makers and publics seek a "peace dividend" in the form of reduced security burdens and the ability to redirect material and intellectual attention toward domestic problems, there is likely to be a measure of frustration with the tendency of international crises to intrude on the public policy agenda. Inevitably, many—perhaps a majority—of these crises will be in the Muslim world or concern relations between Islam and the West.

In the post–Cold War environment instability along the "arc of crisis" running from Morocco to Central Asia has emerged as a leading focus of security concern in its own right—a perception shared in equal measure by observers in Russia as well as the West. This concern has three broad dimensions. First, countries on the Eurasian borderlands are exposed to the spillover effects of instability within the Muslim world as well as regional friction along religious lines. Refugee flows and sporadic interruptions in normal economic and political relations are representative of this dimension. A second aspect concerns the ability of turmoil in the Muslim world to affect global security and prosperity on a *systemic* level, that is, beyond regional consequences. Examples might include the impetus that such instability could give (indeed, is already giving) to the proliferation of weapons of mass destruction and the potential for conflicts over energy supplies affecting the global economy. A third aspect concerns Western frustration with endemic conflict, lack of robust political institutions, and disregard for human rights in the largely Muslim South, and the likely pressure for Western intervention for humanitarian or peacekeeping purposes—a long-term problem with associated risks of engagement *and* disengagement.[42]

In a few cases the potential for confrontation along Muslim-Western lines directly involves the control of territory. Potential flashpoints of this sort include the future of the Spanish enclaves of Ceuta and Melilla on the Moroccan coast and possible competition for control over the Canary Islands. Conflict along Muslim-Christian lines in the Balkans and the Caucasus similarly concerns the control of territory, among other issues, as does the dispute on Cyprus. On the whole, however, territorial issues per se are not a leading feature of security relations between Islam and the West.

Geography itself does play a significant role in shaping security relationships. In the face of instability in the Muslim South and East, the Mediterranean and its hinterlands, including the Balkans, will acquire additional importance as strategic barriers for Europeans. Similarly, Russia may seek to reassert control over regions on its periphery in order to hold perceived sources of instability in the Muslim south at arm's length. This concern over instability in the Muslim "near abroad" has emerged as a leading element in Russian strategic perceptions. To the extent that the influence of conservative, nationalist forces in Moscow expands or even becomes dominant, this attention to the Islamic factor could further deepen with serious implications for the likelihood of Russian confrontation with Iran or Turkey over ethnic frictions in the Caucasus and Central Asia.

The Islamic Factor in European Security

Fear of Islamic instability is likely to play a significant role in the geographic evolution of the European Union and even more clearly in the evolution of European and Atlantic security institutions. Current members of the European Union, particularly France and Germany, are distinctly unwilling to endorse the concept of full Turkish membership, not least because this might eventually imply "European" borders with Syria, Iran, and Iraq. With its latent religious and nationalist pressures—and an active separatist revolt—Turkey is itself part of the problem; the problem in this sense being defined as the risk to Europe from turmoil in the Middle East. Westernized Turks prefer to describe Turkey's strategic role as that of a "bridge" between the Muslim East and the West, between the Middle East and Europe. Europeans, by contrast, are more inclined to view Turkey as a *barrier*; part of the European system, but not fully European.

Movement toward a European defense identity also has certain implications for relations between Europe and the Islamic periphery. Partly as a result of its ambiguous relationship to the North Atlantic Treaty Organization (NATO), and partly as a result of new security concerns, the Western European Union finds its most natural sphere of action in the Mediterranean region. Similarly, the coordination of European surveillance and air defense systems has been most intensive in the South, including the French-Spanish-Italian *Helios* satellite project. None of this has passed unnoticed along the Muslim shores of the Mediterranean, where new European security initiatives are often characterized as being "oriented against us." It is common for observers in North Africa, for example, to view the evolution of new European defense arrangements as a vehicle for intervention in the Muslim world by former colonial powers.

In a transatlantic context, the debate over NATO's future utility and orientation most often concerns the twin challenges of projecting stability eastward and "dealing with the south."[43] The latter invariably includes the problem of Islamic radicalism as a primary or secondary concern. As the alliance adopts a more forward leaning stance on "out-of-area" matters, the potential for NATO's direct involvement in the Muslim south, including the Balkans, will increase. Moreover, discussion of the criteria for membership in an expanded NATO could complicate the position of Muslim Turkey. The suggestion that prospective NATO members in Eastern Europe should first meet the criteria for membership in the European Community is especially troubling for Ankara. More broadly, the accession of additional members from Eastern Europe, possibly even the Balkans and Ukraine, would necessarily bring the alliance into closer contact with the Orthodox-Muslim cleavage (although NATO's role could ultimately be a factor for stability here as in the Greek-Turkish relationship). Observing the discourse over political and security questions in the former communist states of Eastern Europe and central Europe, there is little evidence to suggest that a wider European security grouping will prove more tolerant of perceived threats from the Muslim periphery. Moreover, any NATO expansion is most unlikely to embrace the largely Muslim states of the Caucasus and Central Asia, thus preserving and deepening the definition of the European security space along essentially religious lines.

Proliferation and the North-South Military Balance

Debate over the possible emergence of a new ideological or civilizational conflict between Islam and the West is taking place against the background of established European and U.S. concern about the growth of conventional and unconventional arsenals in the South. For the moment, the ability of Muslim states to pose a direct military threat to Western territory is extremely limited. But the continued acceleration of proliferation trends, spurred on by religious or civilizational frictions, could transform this situation in politically as well as militarily significant ways, presenting Western leaders and strategists with new dilemmas.[44]

For many leading Muslim states the end of the Cold War and the decreasing relevance of alignment as well as nonalignment imply a diminished ability to attract material and political attention and, in more general terms, to be "taken seriously" on the international scene. The new strategic environment is likely to be characterized by a search for alternative vehicles for national prestige and activism. Islam itself may serve this function for some regimes. Others may look to regional integration as a source of weight in international affairs. The search for post–Cold War geopolitical weight is also serving to spur the proliferation of both conventional and unconventional arsenals across the Muslim world. With the prominent exception of North Korea, a leading supplier of ballistic missile and other technologies to the Muslim world, the major proliferators are to be found along an arc from Algeria to Pakistan. As a prominent French observer has noted, "A proper regard for security cannot exclude the hypothesis that several European cities will be— probably sooner than generally expected—the potential targets of these weapons."[45]

Most distant, but also most significant and emotive, is the potential for nuclear proliferation in the Muslim world (that is to say, beyond Pakistan, which is arguably already a nuclear weapons state), especially in light of the dissemination of expertise and nuclear materials resulting from the disintegration of the Soviet Union. Iraq has pursued an active nuclear program, and Iran continues to do so, even reportedly exploring the possibility of purchasing a nuclear device.[46] Syria and Libya have reportedly considered development programs or nuclear purchases. In North Africa, Algeria's ostensibly civilian nuclear program, pursued with Chinese assistance, has been the subject of intense speculation, including allegations that Algeria has cooperated in hiding Iraqi nuclear materials.

Israel's nuclear capability has provided a strong incentive for exploration of the nuclear option in the Muslim world, an incentive that has been reinforced by the disappearance of the Soviet Union as a nuclear guardian, however uncertain. Movement toward a comprehensive settlement between Israel and its Arab neighbors, with all that this might imply for military disengagement, could dampen the dynamics of nuclear proliferation in the region. But the attractiveness of nuclear weapons, even a virtual nuclear capability, as a means of deterring Western intervention and gaining national weight and prestige will remain. In this context, leaderships in the Muslim world surely have contemplated the lessons of the Gulf War along the lines suggested by a senior Indian military leader: "Don't fight the United States unless you have nuclear weapons."[47]

To what extent can these attempts at nuclear or other forms of proliferation be described as a Muslim phenomenon? There has been a certain amount of rhetoric concerning the need for "Islamic" nuclear, chemical, and biological weapons, primarily emanating from Iran. Kazakhstan, for the moment the leading Islamic nuclear power as a result of its retention of ex-Soviet weapons, has been reluctant to disavow the significance of its nuclear capability in relations with the Muslim world.[48] On balance, however, there is little evidence that states within the Muslim world are pursuing the nuclear option in the interests of the Islamic world as a whole, although the prestige accompanying the development of weapons of mass destruction undoubtedly operates in this setting, among others. This also has a vicarious aspect. Tunisia, arguably the country most at risk from Libyan arms, finds itself in the curious position of hedging its concern with observations about the need for an Arab or Islamic deterrent against Israel.[49]

Yet the motives of proliferators within the Muslim world remain, above all, regional and secular. Pakistan's nuclear development has had strategic competition with India as its reference point. Iran had nuclear ambitions before its Islamic revolution, and the Islamic motivations of Iraq, Syria, Libya, or Algeria's FLN are weak at best. The potential for regional proliferation trends to be harnessed explicitly to Muslim aims would require a sense of solidarity and a common sense of threat that, at least at present, does not exist outside the limited (and fading) realm of the confrontation with Israel.

For the moment no Muslim state in the Middle East has the technological capability to *build* long-range ballistic missiles with "militarily significant" accuracy.[50] Current proliferation risks in the ballistic missile as well as the nuclear, chemical, and biological areas stem largely from the increasing availability of technology, materials, and weapons developed elsewhere.[51] Whether the key role of Asian countries as suppliers of nuclear and ballistic missile technology to the Muslim world is the result of a "Confucian-Islamic" strategic connection, as one writer has speculated, or more sensibly, the product of commercial interests, transfers from China and North Korea to South Asia and the Middle East have contributed substantially to the importance of the proliferation factor in relations between Islam and the West.[52] It is noteworthy that the West's confrontation with North Korea over nuclear and ballistic missile programs is not simply about stability on the Korean peninsula or the broader implications of proliferation for the international system. Fear of the spread of North Korean nuclear and ballistic missile technology to the Muslim Middle East and the consequences for European security are frequently mentioned whenever the issue of North Korea is discussed in the Western press.

Syria, Egypt, Libya, Algeria, Iran, Iraq, Saudi Arabia, and Pakistan possess ballistic missiles of varying ranges, and all are seeking to acquire longer-range, more accurate systems.[53] Notably, given the current capabilities based largely on modified Scud missiles, the threat remains largely of a South-South character. Muslim proliferators may talk about the need for Islamic "bombs" and longer-range missiles, but for the moment the chief effect of proliferation trends has been to increase the vulnerability of Muslim states to

Muslim weapons. Because this situation is unlikely to persist, the ballistic missile vulnerability will take on a more pronounced North-South character in Western perceptions as regional powers acquire weapons with trans-Mediterranean ranges.

The 600 km Scud-C missiles already in the possession of Iran, Egypt, and Syria are capable of reaching parts of southern Europe if deployed in Libya or Algeria. Libyan, Algerian, and Iranian negotiations with China and North Korea for missiles with ranges beyond 1,000 km raise the possibility of an entirely different military relationship between Europe and the Muslim world. Such ranges—and ranges of 2,000–3,000 km are conceivable with currently available Asian technology—would place much of Europe, including U.S. military facilities, within reach. The implications for Western freedom of action in responding to crises in the Muslim world could be substantial. As Mu'ammar al-Qadhafi has suggested, "If at the time of the 1986 U.S. raid on Tripoli we had possessed a deterrent missile that could reach New York, we could have hit it at the same moment."[54] Taking into account Libya's missile attack on the Italian island of Lampedusa in retaliation for this same raid, neither Qadhafi's comment nor his willingness to attack closer European targets in response to U.S. actions can be dismissed lightly.

Leaving aside the proliferation of weapons of mass destruction, the proliferation of conventional air and naval systems is a less dramatic but equally important issue for Western security. This trend has been underway for some time, spurred on by the Arab-Israeli confrontation, the Iran-Iraq War, and the more recent conflict in the Gulf. Sales of ships and aircraft from the arsenal of the former Soviet Union, as well as growing pressures for arms exports from the West as domestic markets shrink in the wake of the Cold War are reinforcing factors in this equation. Libyan Su-24 bombers, capable of carrying nuclear or chemical weapons, can reach targets in Italy. Iranian purchases of Backfire bombers and attack submarines from the former Soviet Union are often viewed as giving Tehran a greater ability to deter and coerce regional rivals as well as the West. These developments have considerable symbolic importance, but their significance in terms of the military balance between individual Muslim countries and the West should not be overstated. Unlike the spread of weapons of mass destruction, where symbolism and the risk of use, however slim, is of overwhelming importance, the purchase of advanced conventional weapons does not automatically confer a real increase in military capacity. Modern weapons require a substantial technical infrastructure as well as doctrinal integration to be of real utility in conflict. Few Muslim states possess the technical and industrial resources to use such weapons effectively, even if they are capable of purchasing advanced weapons in meaningful numbers. In the case of Iran, for example, the decline in techno-logical education (more a matter of resources than radical Islamic philoso-phy?) may further complicate the task of integrating modern weaponry with-in the armed forces.

The growing number of suppliers of conventional weapons outside the developed armaments industries of the West also suggests that the capacity of the United States and Europe to limit conflicts within the Muslim world or on its periphery is declining.[55] Indeed, some of the most important suppliers are within the Muslim world itself, including Egypt, Pakistan, and Turkey. The production of F-16 fighters for Egypt in Turkish factories (admittedly with a substantial technical and financial contribution from the United States) is indicative of the sort of arrangements that could become common within the Muslim world.[56]

Muslim arms will flow to Muslim causes. The meaningful question in this regard will continue to be the character of the suppliers. Lifting of the inter-national embargo on arms shipments to the former Yugoslavia would give new freedom of action to Muslim countries of all political inclinations to pro-vide overt support to the Bosnian Muslims. It might also have the effect of redressing the balance between moderate and radical Muslim states in rela-tion to the crisis. Under conditions of embargo, countries such as Iran will continue to act with impunity in their efforts to supply the Muslims, whereas countries such as Turkey will feel bound to act within limits set by interna-tional consensus. With international restrictions reduced or removed, more moderate Muslim states may perceive an opening, even a need, for more overt support.

Arms Control

The prospect of a greater balance of military capability between the Muslim world and the West will have a more direct effect on Europe than on the United States and will be felt most keenly on the European periphery.[57] East-West agreement on the reduction of conventional forces in Europe has left significant arsenals on the European periphery in North Africa and the Middle East unconstrained. At the same time Muslim countries, once leading advocates of regional arms control as a means of reducing the military pres-ence of the superpowers, have adopted a less enthusiastic stance following the disintegration of the Soviet Union. In the wake of the Gulf War, officials and observers in countries as varied as Kazakhstan and Tunisia have been emphasizing the inherent right of smaller and regional powers to acquire the means of self-defense, whether conventional or unconventional. Tentative attempts to explore arms control and confidence-building measures between North and South in the Mediterranean region in the context of the (CSCM) have been set aside pending the results of the Arab-Israeli peace negotiations. As the prospects for a settlement in this area look more promising, the opportunities for reinvigorating the process begun under CSCM may improve. The waning of the confrontation with Israel is likely to remove some, but by no means all, of the rationale for the acquisition of sophisticated arms in the Muslim world. Indeed, serious regional tensions outside the Arab-Israeli context will remain and may take on even new significance. Leading examples include the continuing competition between Iraq and Iran, Syria and Turkey, Libya and Egypt, and Morocco and Algeria. The specific nature of these rivalries and the resulting proliferation pressures argue against the success of sweeping multilateral arms control regimes, although some progress might be made on broadly applicable confidence-building measures.

Other aspects of conventional arms control could just as easily unravel in ways that would heighten tensions between North and South, Islam and the West. In particular, Russian assertions that the CFE limitations may need to be reexamined in light of risks emanating from Muslim regions to the south—"the danger of Islamic fundamentalism along the southern frontier"—are already raising fears of Russian revanchism in Ankara.[58] At the same time, Turkey's military modernization program, including equipment acquired through the "cascading" of CFE surplus arms from Ankara's NATO allies, will have an effect on regional balances beyond the Middle East. Russia, Ukraine, and the Balkan countries, not least Greece, will also be affected by the improvement in the offensive potential of Turkish forces in ways likely to heighten existing awareness of Muslim-Christian fault lines.

Western states will have a growing interest in promoting regional arms control and nonproliferation regimes in the Muslim world. Policy makers and strategists understandably wish to limit the growth of arsenals in the South, because they fear destabilizing effects in the Middle East and, ultimately, risks to the security of the West itself. Given the historic frequency of Western military intervention in the Muslim world, it is not surprising that the West takes a dim view of proliferation trends that might limit its freedom of action. But are Muslim stakes and interests compatible with those of the West when it comes to limiting regional arms? The insecure character of most Muslim regimes and the existence of active competition between states within the Muslim world give tremendous impetus to the proliferation of armaments. This impetus and correspondingly cool attitudes toward arms control are unlikely to be reversed until the security dimension of politics within the Muslim world fades. This could come as a result of political reform, rendering societies more stable and less vulnerable to external threats, or as a result of new and competing economic priorities. In the short term, neither development is likely. Some incentives and a good deal of strategic reassurance may need to come from the West. The disengagement of traditional adversaries within the Muslim world (as well as Israel and its Arab adversaries) will almost certainly require concrete security guarantees from leading Western countries. Thus, a significant degree of Western engagement in the regional security problems of the Muslim world may be a requirement for successful arms limitation and nonproliferation policies.

Access to Resources and Lines of Communication

After a decade of relative obscurity questions of oil supply may be poised to reappear on the Western security agenda (the Gulf crisis briefly raised the specter of price increases and supply interruptions, but these proved ephemeral).[59] With the prospect of expanding demand in Eastern Europe and Asia and declining efficiency in energy use after a prolonged period of low prices, the oil market is likely to become tighter over the next decade. European and U.S. dependence on Middle Eastern oil has quietly grown to historic levels while the prospects for large new reserves are declining everywhere, with the exception of the Middle East itself.[60] In a political context, important new states in the world oil market, notably Kazakhstan and Azerbaijan, may well have more in common with the Muslim members of the Organization of Petroleum Exporting Countries (OPEC) than exporters such as Mexico or Venezuela. All of this suggests—and does no more—that oil could reemerge as a potent political weapon in relations between the Muslim world and the West. No less moderate a commentator than the foreign minister of Turkey has already pointed to the value of Muslim oil "as a weapon to exert direct pressure on the UN Security Council" over the issue of Bosnia.[61] Pressures within the Muslim world itself, including the tension between "rich" oil-producing states and other less well-endowed regimes could play an important role in this regard. To the extent that Islam has become a more potent political force within the Arab world, the oil-producing states of the Gulf may find it difficult to resist widespread calls for use of the oil weapon in future clashes of opinion or arms between Muslim states and the West. A revived Organization of Arab Petroleum Exporting Countries (OAPEC) with a more active Islamic agenda could also encourage more competitive "arms for oil" policies, corrosive of regional stability as well as relations among Western countries.

At the same time the expansion of the infrastructure for the transport of oil and gas to the West and elsewhere will place key borderland states in a critical position. Examples here include Morocco, Spain, and Italy as conduits for North African natural gas and Turkey as a conduit for pipeline-borne oil from the Gulf and, very likely, Azerbaijan. Their position is doubly complicated, since access to energy markets can also be a source of leverage for importers in times of crisis, on the pattern of the continuing ban on Iraqi oil exports through Turkish pipelines to the Persian Gulf. More positively, pipeline networks may also serve to bind together the interests of countries across religious and ethnic divides, with stabilizing effect. This has been the general opinion with regard to the expansion of natural gas transport in the western and central Mediterranean (Tunisia-Sicily). In the East, where the expansion of Central Asian oil and gas exports is a pressing interest, the debate over where new pipelines should or should not be built turns *inter alia* on issues of political risk, not least the perceived unpredictability of the Islamic regime in Teheran.[62] Transport through Turkey, whether by pipeline to terminals on the Mediterranean or via the Black Sea, is emerging as the leading alternative.

As the two recent wars in the Persian Gulf demonstrated, the infrastructure for oil production and export is remarkably resilient. In neither case did deliberate attacks on oil facilities or tankers have the desired effect of wreaking havoc in the world oil market. This will not necessarily stop aggressive regimes from trying, nor will it prevent Western officials and strategists from worrying about the consequences of such attacks. In this context Iran's recent purchase of two ex-Soviet Kilo-class attack submarines (and the possible purchase of a third) cannot fail to arouse some concern about the sea lines of communication for oil, already at risk from mines. It remains as likely that Iran would attempt to employ these weapons to interrupt Iraqi oil exports through the Gulf (should these be resumed) as to attack Western warships. Overall, the risk of a serious disruption in the flow of oil because of attacks on sea routes or infrastructure is probably minimal. The effect on prices and political relations may be more serious.

Access to the Suez Canal has not received much attention as a Western strategic interest or a potential flashpoint in relations between Islam and the West. It is likely to receive more attention on both counts over the next decade. The Suez Canal has lost some of its value as a conduit for oil shipments since the advent of very large crude carriers in the 1960s and 1970s (for much of this time the Suez Canal was unusable). Nonetheless, it remains an extremely important conduit for all sorts of commercial cargo and as such is of particular importance to Russia and Eastern Europe.[63] It has also been essential to the rapid movement of U.S. and European naval and ground forces between the Mediterranean and the Persian Gulf. As the size of the permanent U.S. naval presence in both regions declines as a result of post–Cold War reductions, the ability to shift forces from the Atlantic and Europe to the Persian Gulf and Indian Ocean is likely to become even more critical. Yet unimpeded access to the Suez Canal for this purpose depends on the acquiescence of the Egyptian government. It is not beyond imagination that even the current regime in Cairo, much less an Islamic government, would close the Suez Canal to Western intervention forces in solidarity with other Muslim states or even as an act of considered neutrality.

International Terrorism

The phenomena of political violence and radical Islam are closely connect-ed in Western perceptions, and in a more general sense, the sponsors and stakes of international terrorism are seen as largely Muslim and Middle Eastern. In reality, terrorism of an overtly Islamic character represents only a fraction of the world total, but its impact is considerable as a result of its lethality. Since 1982 Shi'ite Islamic groups have been responsible for roughly 8 percent of all international terrorist incidents, yet these incidents accounted for 30 percent of the total number of deaths.[64] Whereas secular terrorist groups normally view indiscriminate violence as counterproductive, religious extremists—and Islamic groups are by no means the only movements in this category—see fewer political and moral constraints on the use of violence. Their use of terror has been described as having a transcendental dimension, in which aims are sweeping and the category of potential enemies open-ended.[65] The lethality of radical Muslim terrorism is an important aspect of its prominence in Western perceptions. Another aspect, perhaps more significant from the foreign and security policy perspective, has been the prominence of Muslim regimes in "state-sponsored" terrorism. Iran, Libya, and Syria have all been active on this front, with Sudan and Iraq alleged to be at the center of several recent incidents. Afghanistan too has emerged from its struggle with Soviet occupation into a period of turmoil in which veterans of the Afghan resistance, and many who identify themselves as such but never really fought there, form a notable presence within radical Islamic movements across the Middle East. Their role in political violence in such places as Algeria and Egypt is hotly debated in both the Muslim world and the West.

Western policy makers will continue to face the prospect of Middle Eastern and Islamic terrorism within their own borders, on the pattern of the bombing of Pan Am Flight 103 in 1988 or the World Trade Center bombing of 1993, as well as violence aimed at their nationals and institutions abroad. With the end of the Cold War and movement toward an Arab-Israeli settlement, the agenda of Middle Eastern terrorism may change substantially. Religious extremists on both sides may emerge as the most violent opponents of any Palestinian settlement and may bring their battle to Europe and the United States. A sense of Western abandonment among Bosnia's Muslims and the prospect of a Bosnian diaspora could stimulate the creation of new terrorist groups, possibly with state backing from elsewhere in the Muslim world. Established state-sponsored groups such as the Iranian-supported Party of God have expanded their network of operations in North and South America, as well as North Africa.[66] The likelihood of Iranian involvement in new terrorist incidents in the United States and Europe will, among other things, worsen the prospects for a rapprochement between Washington and Teheran.

Terrorist violence against officials and secular intellectuals, whether threats against Salman Rushdie or the assassination of leading figures in Egypt and Algeria, has become a feature of radical Islamic opposition movements in North Africa and elsewhere. The deepening of antisecular violence and the equally violent reaction from security forces threaten the stability of regimes in which the West has a strong security interest. It is not inconceivable that Islamic radicals, who may or may not be successful in bringing about the overthrow of secular governments in Algiers or Cairo, will choose to intensify terror campaigns in the open, more vulnerable societies of the West. Even in Italy, where domestic and international terrorism have long posed a challenge to state and society, officials have been especially outspoken on the problem of Islamic violence, despite their desire to preserve workable relations with Iran and Libya.[67]

Overall, the thrust of international terrorism in its Middle Eastern dimension is changing as an older generation of activists inspired by the Palestinian issue and opposition to Israel (e.g., the Popular Front for the Liberation of Palestine) gives way to groups with an Islamic agenda such as Islamic Jihad and Hamas.[68] In this context, the significance of the so-called Afghani or veterans of the guerrilla war against the Soviet occupation of Afghanistan, noted in the Algerian and Egyptian cases, may have more to do with their role as symbols of politically alienated Muslim youth than their weight in numbers or ferocity (many of the "Afghani" active in the Islamic opposition movement in Algeria never actually fought in Afghanistan).[69] Moreover, the spread of weapons from the Afghan resistance could have serious consequences for the lethality of international terrorism. Stinger missiles, capable of bringing down commercial aircraft, and other weapons from Afghanistan are reportedly being sold to groups in Central Asia, the Indian subcontinent, and the Middle East.

The prominence of radical Islamic terrorism in Western perception may also influence the extent and the character of the U.S. and European role in peacekeeping operations, many of which are likely to be conducted in Muslim countries (see discussion below). Policy makers cannot fail to be sensitive to the vulnerabilities suggested by the bombing of the U.S. Marine headquarters in Lebanon or the more recent attacks on Italian troops in Somalia.[70] More broadly, it will be difficult to envision any form of intervention in the Muslim world without considering the possibility of retaliatory terrorist attacks. The likelihood that Western powers will find cause for intervention in the Muslim world, perhaps frequent intervention, suggests that radical Islamic terrorism and responses to it will be a fixture of the strategic environment for some time to come. It may even be argued that the failure of Islamic opposition movements to become normal participants in the political process across the Muslim world increases the risk of terrorist violence as frustrated extremists seek international outlets for their activism. In this as in other ways, Western security will be directly affected by political turmoil in the Muslim South.

Notes

1. See Timothy Sisk, *Islam and Democracy: Religion, Politics and Power in the Middle East* (Washington, D.C.: U.S. Institute of Peace, 1992); and Laura Guazzone. "Democracy, Stability and the Islamist Phenomenon in North Africa," paper prepared for RAND-IAI conference, "The New Mediterranean Security Environment: Regional Issues and Responses," Washington, D.C., February 18–19, 1993.

2. See, for example, Mernissi, *Islam and Democracy;* and Sisk, *Islam and Democracy.*

3. Judith Miller. "The Challenge of Radical Islam," *Foreign Affairs,* Spring 1993, p. 45.

4. This phenomenon is discussed at length in Alvin Z. Rubinstein and

Pauline Soliman, "America in Egypt's Press," *Mediterranean Quarterly*, Spring 1994.

5. See, for example, Leon T. Hadar, "What Green Peril?" *Foreign Affairs*, Spring 1993.

6. See discussion in Claire Spencer, *The Maghreb in the 1990s*, Adelphi Paper No. 274 (London: IISS, 1993); and Remy Leveau, *Algeria: Adversaries in Search of Uncertain Compromises*, Chaillot Paper No. 4 (Paris: Western European Union Institute for Security Studies, 1992); and Ian O. Lesser, *Security in North Africa: Internal and External Challenges* (Santa Monica: RAND, 1993).

7. See Steven A. Holmes, "Iran's Shadow: Fundamentalism Alters the Mideast's Power Relationships," *New York Times*, August 22, 1993.

8. See, for example, Tony Walker, "Egypt Fearful of Iran's Influence over Sudan," *Financial Times*, December 17, 1991.

9. See Martin Kramer, "Islam vs. Democracy," *Commentary*, January 1993.

10. William Drozdiak, "Intellectuals Being Killed in Algeria," *Washington Post*, June 27, 1993.

11. It is estimated that the populations of Turkey and Egypt in the year 2025 will reach 100 million each, and that of the five states of the AMU—Mauritania, Morocco, Algeria, Tunisia, and Libya—will total 127 million. The population of these seven countries combined will roughly equal that of the current European Community. See Gil Loescher, "Refugee Movements and International Security," *Adelphi Paper* No. 268 (London: IISS, Summer 1992), p. 21; and George Joffe and Kurt Gasteyger papers on "European Security and the New Arc of Crisis," in "New Dimensions in International Security," *Adelphi Paper* No. 265 (London: IISS, Winter 1991/92), p. 62.

12. Giorgio Gomel, "Migrations toward Western Europe: Trends, Outlook, Policies," *International Spectator* (Rome), April-June 1992, pp. 76–77.

13. Muslim populations in Europe include some 2 million in France 2 million in Germany, 1 million in Britain, and 500,000 in Spain. Hadar, "What Green Peril?" p. 28. Estimates of the total North African population in Western Europe range as high as 6 million. Loescher, "Refugee Movements and International Security," p. 21.

14. See Henry Kamm, "Migrants Wear out Welcome as Numbers Grow in Europe," *New York Times*, February 10, 1993.

15. Perhaps a third of the Turkish population in Germany is of Kurdish descent.

16. "Spanish authorities warn that if the Community does nothing, the Maghreb will end up exploding, and we cannot, they say, stop its shock waves from reaching us. The whole of Europe would then be affected." "EC, Morocco Discuss Fishing Rights, Maghreb," *FBIS-WEU,* March 2, 1992.

17. For example, increasingly restrictive Spanish immigration policy could inflame opinion in Morocco, with negative consequences for the stability of the Spanish enclaves of Ceuta and Melilla. See Oliver Wilcox, "Spain and Morocco: Ceuta, Melilla and Immigration," *Middle East International,* April 30, 1993.

18. See Loescher, "Refugee Movements and International Security."

19. There has been a distinct revival of Islamic practice among the majority Muslim population of Albania as well as traditionally secular Bosnia. See Henry Kamm, "Albania's Clerics Lead a Rebirth," *New York Times,* March 27, 1992.

20. Bassma Kodmani-Darwish, "International Security and the Forces of Nationalism and Fundamentalism," in *New Dimensions in International Security,* Adelphi Paper No. 266 (London: IISS, Winter 1991/92), p. 45.

21. See Nicholas X. Rizopoulos, "A Third Balkan War?" *World Policy Journal,* Summer 1993.

22. See "Non-Aligned Move to Lift Arms Embargo on Muslims," *Turkish Daily News,* May 24, 1993; "Islamic Conference Meeting on Bosnia Concludes," FBIS-NES, December 4, 1992, p. 1.

23. Serbian estimates are, not surprisingly, much higher. Chuck Sudetic, "Muslims from Abroad Join in War against Serbs," *New York Times,* November 14, 1992.

24. Stephen Engelberg, "Degree Varies as Arabs Assist Bosnia's Muslims." *New York Times,* August 23, 1992.

25. "Izetbegovic Calls for Support from Islamic States," *FBIS-EEU,* January 6, 1992, p. 5.

26. Franjo Tudjman, the Croatian president, has stated that "the division of Bosnia-Herzegovina into Serb, Croat and Muslim communities was inevitable because Europe would not tolerate a unitary Islamic state in its

midst." Cited in Engelberg, "Degree Varies."

27. See Sudetic, "Muslims from Abroad"; and Ghassan Salame, "Islam and the Westy" *Foreign Policy,* Spring 1993, p. 28.

28. Caryle Murph, "West Has Helped Fuel New Islamic Militancy," *Washington Post,* May 1, 1993.

29. Alan Riding, "Paris Journal: For the Bosnian Cause, Some French Brainpower," *New York Times,* May 26, 1994.

30. The reality may be otherwise. A prominent observer argues that religion is not per se a primary cause of Azeri-Armenian hostility or the conflict over Abkhazia. Paul B. Henze, *Conflict in the Caucasus* (Santa Monica, CA: RAND, P-7830, 1993), pp. 7–8.

31. See Graham E. Fuller, *Central Asia: The New Geopolitics* (Santa Monica, CA: RAND, 1992).

32. See Philip Shenon, "Non-Aligned Movement Decides It Is Still Relevant," *New York Times,* September 2, 1992; and "Non-Aligned Movement Holds Talks on Finding a New Reason for Being," *New York Times,* September 7, 1992.

33. Edward Mortimer, "New Fault Lines: Is a North-South Confrontation Inevitable in Security Terms?" in *New Dimensions in International Security,* Adelphi Paper No. 266 (London: IISS, Winter 1991/92), p. 77.

34. See Winrich Kuhne and Stefan Mair, *European-African Relations: Challenges in the 1990s* (Ebenhausen: Stiftung Wissenschaft und Politik, October 1992).

35. See James A. Winnefeld and Mary E. Morris, *Where Environmental Concerns and Security Strategies Meet: Green Conflict in Asia and the Middle East,* MR-378-RC [Santa Monica: RAND, 1994].

36. See Robert Lempert and Gwen Farnsworth, "Environmental Security in the Mediterranean," in Ian Lesser and Robert Levine, eds., *The RAND/Istituto Affari Internazionali Conference on the New Mediterranean Security Environment* (Santa Monica, CA: RAND, CF-110-RC, 1993).

37. See Claude Lorieux, "Unification et Europe: Les Défis du Maghreb." *Figaro,* July 27, 1990; and Francis Ghiles, "Maghreb States Seek to Strengthen Ties with EC," *Financial Times,* July 25, 1990.

38. See Lesser, *Security in North Africa.*

39. Mortimer, "New Fault Lines," p. 81.

40. Dominique Moisi, quoted in Judith Miller, "Strangers at the Gate: Europe's Immigration Crisis," *New York Times,* September 15, 1991, p. 86.

41. Mortimer, *European Security after the Cold War,* p. 36.

42. See Adam Roberts, "Humanitarian War: Military Intervention and Human Rights," *International Affairs* (London), July 1993.

43. See, for example, Ronald Asmus, Richard Kugler, and F. Stephen Larrabee, "Building a New NATO," *Foreign Affairs,* September/October 1993.

44. For contrasting European and Maghrebi perceptions, see Mustapha Sehimi, "La Sécurité en Mediterranée Occidentale: Une Approche Maghrebine," and Roberto Aliboni, "La Sécurité Militaire en Mediterranée Occidentale: Le Point de Vue Européen." in Alvaro Vasconcelos, ed., *Européens et Maghrébins: Une Solidarité Obligée* (Paris: Karthala, 1993).

45. Pierre Lellouche, "France in Search of Security." *Foreign Affairs,* Spring 1993, p. 124.

46. See "Algeria and the Bomb," *The Economist,* January 11, 1992, p. 11; and Jack Nelson, "Fears Grow That Soviet A-Arms Are On the Market," *Los Angeles Times,* January 11, 1992.

47. An extensive analysis of the diplomatic, strategic, and technical lessons of the Gulf War can be found in Patrick J. Garrity, *Why the Gulf War Still Matters: Foreign Perspective on the War and the Future of International Security* (Los Alamos: Center for National Security Studies, 1993).

48. "NATO's Southern Tier: A Strategic Risk Appraisal," *European Security,* Spring 1993, p. 53.

49. Lesser, *Security in North Africa,* p. 67.

50. See Maurizio Cremasco, "Perspectives on the International Scene at the Start of 1993," paper presented at RAND-IAI conference, "The New Mediterranean Security Environment," Washington, D.C., February 18–19, 1993, p. 18.

51. It is estimated that upwards of fourteen Third World countries have a chemical weapons capability, including Iran, Iraq, Pakistan, Syria, and Egypt. Algeria is thought to possess the technical infrastructure to develop chemical weapons if it wished.

52. Huntington, "The Clash of Civilizations?"

53. On regional trends in missile proliferation see Aaron Karp, "Ballistic Missile Proliferation," in *SIPRI Yearbook, 1991, World Armaments and Disarmament* (New York: Oxford University Press, 1991); Janne Nolan, *The Trappings of Power: Ballistic Missiles in the Third World* (Washington, D.C.: Brookings, 1991); and Martin Navias. "Ballistic Missile Proliferation in the Third World," *Adelphi Paper* No. 252 (London: IISS, 1990).

54. Address published in *FBIS-MEA*, April 23, 1990; also cited in Uzi Rubin, "How Much Does Missile Proliferation Matter?" *Orbis,* Winter 1991.

55. Steven R. David, "Why the Third World Still Matters," *International Security,* Winter 1992/93, p. 148.

56. Egypt is currently negotiating the purchase of forty F-16s manufactured in Turkey. See "Paper Notes Egyptian Position on F-16 Purchases," *FBIS-WEU,* February 24, 1992, p. 43. Another, somewhat different example is provided by the security agreement between Sudan and Iran, under which Iran will subsidize Khartoum's purchase of $260 million worth of Chinese arms. See "Iran, Sudan, Form Strategic Alliance," *Mednews,* February 3, 1992.

57. See Roberto Aliboni, *European Security across the Mediterranean,* Chaillot Paper No. 2 (Paris: Western European Union Institute for Security Studies, 1991), p. 6; and Laura Guazzone, "Threats from the South and the Security of Southern Europe," paper presented at the Portuguese Institute for International and Strategic Studies Tenth Anniversary Conference, Lisbon, November 8–10, 1990, pp. 13–15.

58. The Russian request was conveyed to Secretary of Defense Aspin and has been restarted since by the Russian minister of defense, Pavel Grachev, in May 1993. Michael R. Gordon, "Russia, Worried by South, Asks Arms Pact Change," *New York Times,* May 11, 1993.

59. Some readers will object that the Gulf intervention was itself a product of oil supply concerns. This *might* have been true in the early stages of the crisis, but it was soon overshadowed by broader interests and objectives. See Ian O. Lesser, *Oil, the Persian Gulf and Grand Strategy: Contemporary Issues in Historical Perspective* (Santa Monica, CA: RAND, R-4072, 1991).

60. For a recent assessment see Joseph Stanislaw and Daniel Yergin, "Oil: Reopening the Door," *Foreign Affairs,* September/October 1993; see also Edward Morse, "The Coming Oil Revolution," *Foreign Affairs,* Winter 1990/1991.

For a dissenting view on the issue of scarcity, now somewhat dated, see Julian Simon, *The Ultimate Resource* (Princeton, NJ: Princeton University Press, 1981).

61. Foreign Minister Hikmet Cetin in an interview given to *Hurriyet*, quoted by Reuters, January 7, 1993.

62. "Super Pipelines for Europe," *Foreign Report* (London), August 5, 1993, pp.3–4.

63. On European maritime interests generally, see *Europe's Maritime Interests: Conference Report and Proceedings* (Ebenhausen: Stiftung Wissenschaft und Politik, August 1991).

64. As analyzed in *RAND Chronology of International Terrorism*. See Bruce Hoffman, *Terrorist Targeting: Tactics, Trends, and Potentialities* (Santa Monica, CA: RAND, P-7801, 1992), p. 7.

65. Ibid. pp. 8–9; and David C. Rapoport, "Fear and Trembling: Terrorism in Three Religious Traditions," *American Political Science Review*, September 1984, p. 674.

66. Douglas Fehl, "Iran-backed Terrorists Are Growing More Aggressive, U.S. Warns," *New York Times*, March 18, 1993.

67. Interior Minister Nicolo Mancino has stated, "Let it be quite clear that the main terrorist threat we face comes from Islamic fundamentalism." Interview on state radio, cited in Charles Richards, "Italy Warns West of Islamic Conspiracy," *Independent*, March 19, 1993.

68. See Mouna Naim, "Islamists Change Face of Middle Eastern Terrorism," *Le Monde*, May 29, 1993, in *The Guardian Weekly*, June 6, 1993.

69. Perhaps 15–20,000 Muslim volunteers from abroad fought with the Afghan resistance over the course of the conflict.

70. See Kenneth B. Noble, "Islamic Ire Festering in Somalia," *New York Times*, January 15, 1993.

5

CONTEMPORARY DILEMMAS POSED TO THE ISLAMIC WORLD BY THE WEST

The Islamic world feels itself under siege from the West in numerous vital political, military, cultural, social, and economic realms. This feeling of siege has several sources: the perception of victimization and Western onslaught based on historical and psychological grounds, as discussed earlier; "objective" internal pressures generated by the process of modernization and related social and economic tensions (although the process of modernization is largely unavoidable, its negative consequences are often blamed on the West); and conscious, direct pressure from the West in the policy arena.

Political Pressures

Muslim states face strong political pressures from the West in several ways. First, there are pressures to resolve the Arab-Israeli problem. In fact, most Muslim states and populations would like to be rid of the Arab-Israeli problem. It has been an albatross around the necks of many regimes for nearly five decades. Radical Arab leaders have, of course, often benefited from the conflict by exploiting it to compel moderate states into more uncompromising "Arab nationalist" positions that strengthen the radicals. Dictators have used the issue domestically to demand "vigilance" and the elimination of liberties in the name of the "struggle against the Zionist enemy." Nonradical Arab states thus have some incentive to remove this issue from the agenda of the radicals. At the same time, the moral weight of the Palestinians' dilemma in the eyes of the Muslim public has also placed non-ignorable demands upon Arab leaders to support the Palestinian cause in one way or another.

Western states, especially the United States, have placed unremitting pressure upon the Muslim world to accept and deal with Israel. The friendship and support of the United States has been meted out to Middle Eastern states in close accordance with this main issue. And for all the reasons discussed in Chapter 3, in the eyes of Muslim and especially Arab publics Israel has been the paramount source of national humiliation and the defining issue of national sovereignty and independence from Western pressure—linked with repeated military defeat. Muslim publics have thus experienced the Israeli issue as the chief facet of relations with Washington and the key source of Western political intervention. These are visceral issues, for they relate directly to Muslim soil and Muslim refugees.

In military terms, as noted in the previous section, the Muslim world has also been a leading arena for Western military intervention designed to compel action. This reality is compounded by continuing Western efforts to maintain a military presence in many parts of the region, a presence welcomed by few populations, even if assented to by some rulers as a means of strengthening their own authority and domestic security. At various times Western bases in Egypt, Libya, Saudi Arabia, Oman, Iran, Jordan, Bahrain, Morocco, Turkey, and Pakistan have been viewed generally by regional elites as Western infringement upon their sovereignty designed to further Western, not their own, strategic goals.[1] The elites and the masses, as opposed to ruling families or regimes, do not usually perceive major threats to themselves from neighbors; indeed, they have tended to see Israel as the state most likely to attack them. Thus, there has generally been widespread popular sympathy among populations of the region for the targets of Western attack, such as Qadhafi and Saddam Hussein, simply because they are seen as victims of the regular exercise of Western superior military power.

Economic Frictions

Frictions with the West in the economic realm are even more complex and often reflect broader North-South frictions over economic relations of inequality. They also reflect anxiety and defensiveness about an ability to cope with the realities of a new economic order in the Middle East after an Arab-Israeli peace settlement that, it is feared, will be dominated by Israel at Arab expense.

In principle the possession of massive oil and energy reserves should give many of the states of the Middle East a sense of power and equality in dealing with the West. In fact, however, Muslim oil states have only over the last two decades wrested from the West the right to fully possess and control their own resources. For most of the century and before, these oil resources were viewed as so essential to Western economies that Muslim governments had very little voice or control over the disposition of their own resources. Ownership of oil franchises, companies, and pricing policies were controlled by the outside; local governments in the region risked overthrow if they did not cooperate. Thus native control over these resources has only recently been realized. Muslims are well aware that this relationship has hardly been one of equality, mutual respect, or even commercial convenience, but essentially a colonial one. For this reason Islamists speak of reestablishment of control over their own resources as the "second phase" of an ongoing three-stage decolonization process. (Phase 3 is "cultural decolonization.")

Even then, possession of a critical and strategic international resource has ironically spelled not greater national sovereignty for its owners but actually diminished sovereignty. The critical economic nature of the commodity requires its possessor to cede a large element of control over its disposition—how much to sell and how much to sell it for. No other international commodity is so compromising to the sovereignty of its possessor. The Saudi-imposed oil embargo of 1973–1974—the only time it has been invoked in the region, and by an ally, not an enemy, of the West—unleashed strong passions in the West, whose tolerance for the least degree of foreign dependency is low, and sparked talk of Western use of the "food weapon" as a riposte to the Middle Eastern "oil weapon."

Indeed, this very confrontation raised broader questions about food security in the region and particularly sparked in Saudi Arabia the determination to adopt elaborate and costly schemes of irrigation to grow wheat—at vastly greater cost than the market price. In a speech at the UN in 1975 President Ford referred to the possibility of linking food to oil prices; Henry Kissinger spoke of the possibility of U.S. intervention in the oil fields in the event of "some actual strangulation of the industrialized world," the truculence of which deeply angered the Arabs and even the Shah of Iran.[2] These remarks were followed shortly by enunciation of the Carter doctrine that spelled out the use of force by the United States if necessary to deter "an attempt by any outside force to gain control of the Persian Gulf"—a statement of explicit regional dominance by the West that disturbed the entire Gulf region, including U.S. allies Saudi Arabia and Kuwait.[3] These assertions in effect posited virtual permanent regional vulnerability to U.S. power, particularly vexing when the Soviet threat in the Gulf—the pretext for Western action—was in Arab eyes virtually nonexistent.

Apart from ownership and control of resources, the broader and even more difficult problem of commodity prices and the Third World's vulnerability to their fluctuation bear a direct relation to oil prices. It was the Shah of Iran, a close U.S. ally, who suggested that oil in the 1970s was grossly underpriced for such a "noble element," which should be reserved for the manufacture of petrochemicals rather than crudely burned. To this day the Muslim world remains convinced that Western policies are basically dedicated to manipulation of Middle Eastern politics in order to "gain control of the oil." For example, the argument is popularly invoked that the United States "set up" Saddam Hussein in 1990 to encourage him to invade Kuwait in order to then justify a massive U.S. invasion and the establishment of a permanent military presence—a U.S. goal that in regional eyes has now been largely accomplished. United States interest in Kazakhstan is explained by most Muslims exclusively in terms of oil. United States intervention in Somalia was driven primarily by an interest in "Somali oil reserves," as explained in much of the Arab press. In short, there is a Muslim paranoia relating to oil, its importance to the West, and its role as source of persistent Western intervention.

The economies of the Muslim world are perceived as deeply connected to the West and its powerful economic institutions. Beyond mere financial control, the region discerns a more fundamental "cultural gap" that leads to friction with the West in the economic and social realm. A basic dichotomy is revealed in the Muslim perception: an American vision of a society designed to function on the basis of efficient capitalist principles, as opposed to a Muslim predisposition (common to most traditional societies) to organize government and society to meet certain ethical, social, and religious goals involving the social interests of all classes, including the poor. (That the actual practice of the economies of many Muslim states reveals limited social compassion is overlooked in favor of this Muslim ideal.) Clashes between these priorities become less theoretical and more practical when financial institutions such as the IMF become involved in the problem. As a result, the clash is between the social and economic interests of the population, on the one hand, and the financial requirements of international institutions, on the other. A volatile atmosphere is created in which Western institutions with their policies of "conditionality" readily appear as instruments of Muslim social hardship.

The IMF in particular is cited as imposing a narrow economic orthodoxy on the governments and economies of many Third World states, pushing them toward politically disastrous austerity policies that threaten broader social stability, starting with cuts in subsidies to the basic retail commodities of bread, cooking oil, and sugar, cuts that deeply affect the poor. Economic reform, "open door" policies, and privatization are seen as opening the door only to the growth of a narrow new mercantile nouveau riche, growing gaps between rich and poor, and greater inflation with disastrous effects on the lower and middle classes already living on the margins. States that for years have been committed to fulfillment of an unspoken social contract with the public—social and economic security in exchange for political passivity—now find it ever more difficult to fulfill the economic end of that social bargain. Inefficient government-owned industries fulfill a measure of social security functions in providing employment regardless of need or efficiency. Government bureaucracies provide regular sinecures to college graduates who might not otherwise find employment. Reform, privatization, and a move toward greater efficiency thus have potentially massive social costs that few governments are willing to risk. Privatization is often perceived as selling out to private interests that grow rich without regard for social obligations. In short, the clash of economic and social priorities is sharp—and familiar even in the West or in the reform problems of Russia and Eastern Europe.

Most political forces in the Muslim world are committed to a social rather than economic vision of society. Groups that perceive free enterprise as the path to a better future are small and lack influence. It was the intellectual left that came to power nearly everywhere after the end of colonialism, and although the leftists are now perceived to have historically failed in meeting the postindependence needs of their societies and states, the Islamists, now poised to replace them, have no less a social vision than the left. The Islamists' economic and social policies give priority to moral vision and principles rather than to purely economic concerns. This gives them a strong predisposition to a populist economic policy.

Neither Islam nor the Islamists have any basic hostility to the free market or to business activities per se. The prophet Muhammad was a merchant himself, after all, and the early Islamic state was steeped in mercantile principles. The fact remains, however, that Islamists are competing for power in a political environment in which the nationalists and socialists of the postindependence generation have failed to meet the economic and social needs of society. Islamists who are elected or otherwise come to power will be required to meet high expectations and to swiftly assuage existing economic grievances and hardships. Realistically, the Islamists will face immense pressure to adopt a populist set of policies. A policy of drastic economic reforms, a la IMF, can hardly be expected to emerge in this political environment, even if there is no inherent Islamic hostility to market forces.[4]

In general, however, it is difficult to imagine that Islamist governments, once in power, will be able to resist pressures to turn immediately to the resources of the state to meet the needs of the bulk of the population. The Sudanese case notwithstanding, they will likely reject any externally imposed economic austerity program or debt requirements, at least in the short term, and will be ideologically predisposed to denouncing such Western pressures as hostile, alien, and counterproductive to their own political needs. This real clash of interests is likely to be expressed in terms of "Islam versus the West." Indeed, nearly all governments in the region will find it difficult to resist externalizing the blame for economic tensions within society. And deterioration of political relations with the West will inevitably spill over into economic relations, as was the case in Sudan.

Arab-Israeli Peace: Facing the New Economic Order

The prospects for a comprehensive peace agreement between Israel and its Arab neighbors are at their most promising since the conflict began. Despite the clear-cut benefits that this peace will bring to the region—not least of all to Arab states that have spent billions of dollars on arms over the decades, ostensibly to counter Israel—the outlook is not universally positive to all Arab observers. Unfortunately, the legacy of imperialism, historical loss of self-confidence, and defensiveness against the external world stimulate deep concern and paranoia on the part of many Arab intellectuals who see the new world order in the Middle East as dominated by the United States and by an Israel that not only maintains its stunning military superiority but through the process of political normalization is now positioned to develop an economic hegemony over the region as well. The fear is that Israeli capital and technology will now be able to successfully penetrate Arab markets, and dominate regional trade at the expense of Arab enterprises.

One Bahraini columnist writes that

> the prospects of Arab-Israeli normalization sets alarm bells ringing....The new Middle Eastern order [can be characterized] as one in which the Arabs are being browbeaten into accepting Israeli domination, surrendering their rights and swallowing their pride in the process....The "bills" of the new order [include] the incessant westward drain of Arab resources and of political and social repression. The "spoils" are destined for the pockets of a tiny minority, while the majority suffer from mounting poverty, want and repression.

An Egyptian Islamist writes that the Palestinian-Israeli declaration is in reality "an economic agreement under political cover....Israel hopes to use the accord to "penetrate" the entire Arab world, indeed the entire Middle East....[The agreement] is Israel's first step towards the 'Middle East market' it has been dreaming of."[5]

More optimistic observers see opportunity in the future for the Arab world and urge positive and realistic approaches to future change.

> The [Israeli-Palestinian Declaration of Principles signed in September 1993] has ended Arab-Jewish enmity and defused the conflict forever....Those groups which seek to resist this transformation by "harking back to old slogans"—be they Islamist or Arab nationalist—are "swimming against the tide" and doing their best to ensure that the change is as problematic as they can make it....It is vital for the Arabs to prepare themselves psychologically to accept Israel in their midst and do business with it while ignoring the taboos of the past. [The new era will be characterized] by an Arab-Israel political rapprochement, trade relations, an end to the Arab economic boycott of Israel, increasing Arab-Israeli cooperation against "terrorism," and a flow of investment capital across the former Arab-Israel battle-lines.[6]

Similarly, an Egyptian commentator states that

> Arab fears of being economically swamped by Israel in a future "Middle East Common Market" are largely misplaced. The conditions for such a market being developed simply do not exist, and warnings of Israeli domination are for the most part being made by opponents or critics of the peace process acting out of political motives rather than as a result of a considered analysis of the economic consequences.[7]

Many Arab commentators, then, while resigned to the peace process, are fearful that it represents another step in the Western-imposed forced march toward a new international order in which the Arab world will again be the loser.

Migration

Virtually all Muslim non-oil states today have become heavily dependent on the export of labor to the oil states for remittances that play a crucial role in the hard-currency earnings of the state. The Muslim world, particularly the Maghreb states and Turkey, views emigration and close economic integration with Western Europe as critical to their financial well-being, as a source of hard-currency remittances, and as a safety valve on the labor market. Thus there is extreme anxiety in the Muslim world about prospects for the closure of European labor markets under new European Community regulations. Muslims see themselves as particularly targeted as "undesirables," especially as they witness the anti-immigration jingoism of rightist politicians in France, Italy, and Germany and the attacks on Muslim "guest-workers."

Emigration is not only an economic issue but a social one as well. As the number of Muslim communities in Western Europe grows and the communities take root, Europeans raise major social questions about the degree of Muslim "assimilability" into European society. Indeed, assimilation is not always a goal of the immigrant community that seeks to maintain much of its own traditions and values intact.

Islamic Communities Abroad

The existence of more Muslim communities in the West presents one of the most important cultural challenges to Islam in the next century. For it is precisely in this interplay between the two cultures that some of the most basic issues between Islam and the West will or will not be reconciled and resolved. On the one hand, Islamic communities in the West will try to retain their conservative social philosophy and to preserve their values in the Western community. On the other hand, with each generation it will prove increasingly difficult to maintain these practices. Muslim immigrant parents will have problems holding their teenagers to traditional social patterns as the children push for greater assimilation with Western lifestyles and attitudes.[8] It will be nearly impossible for Islam to play the formal institutional role in daily life in a non-Muslim setting. Indeed, Islam in the West is also likely to become more "secularized," that is, set apart from the government and social institutions, and to evolve increasingly into the expression of personal faith and conduct rather than a set of laws for society. In short, the presence of Islam in the West may hasten its move toward a process similar to the Christian Reformation.

At the heart of the encounter lies the issue of preservation of a religious-cultural community in the face of Western cultural onslaught. What kinds of compromises can be reached that will preserve Muslim cultural values and yet enable Muslim communities to accept broader international norms and be part of the international community? For the politically dedicated

Islamist, a Muslim existence within a Western community is almost a contradiction in terms because a Muslim political environment is almost technically required to facilitate the ability to lead a Muslim life within the precepts of the Shari'a (Islamic law). Life for the Muslim in a non-Muslim society is thus viewed in Islamic terms as presenting special hardships and special problems. In strict traditional terms, a Muslim should emigrate out of a non-Muslim society if possible.

This problem has been faced throughout the history of Islam but in modern times it has been posed most directly by the experience of nearly 100 million Muslims coming under Hindu domination in India after independence and partition in 1947. For the first time in Islamic history a huge body of Muslims now had to live in a secular and non-Muslim society that drew no legal distinctions between religious communities.[9]

It was no longer even a question of undertaking a movement to "attain freedom," for Muslims technically had legal freedom. This unprecedented situation has forced the massive community of Indian Muslims to face new realities about their permanent situation in a secular society, in which they are largely "ghettoized."[10]

That problem is recreated today with the growing presence of Muslims in Western Europe and the United States. How do Muslims adapt to living in a non-Muslim society? Western society is, of course, secular, but this environment is actually preferable for Muslims in the West: All religious minorities in any state prefer secular society they are not discriminated against as a religious minority. For that matter, most Muslims in fact live in considerably secularized societies in the Middle East as well, even if these societies avoid describing themselves as such. In reality most Muslim states operate on the basis of European legal systems in which Islamic precepts mainly affect only what is called "family law." These societies are, of course, culturally Muslim, so that the practice of Islam, religious holidays, fasting during Ramadan, teaching of Islam in schools, and so on, are part of legally recognized public life and to that extent not fully secular.

But the crisis before Muslim society at large remains: Can it remain genuinely Muslim within secular society when state and social mechanisms are not dedicated to the preservation, protection, and extension of Islamic custom and when the dominant cultural values and traditions are non-Muslim? The experience of Muslims living in the West within fully secular societies will profoundly influence the ways that Muslims come to think about secular society in general. The experience is even likely to facilitate and hasten broader transition to secular patterns in the Middle East itself.

In blunt terms, Islam in the West faces two basic alternatives: Euro-Islam or ghetto-Islam.[11] Euro-Islam implies the choice of full Muslim integration into European society (to the extent Europeans socially permit it) while preserving Islam as a matter of personal faith and cultural preference. The alternative, ghetto-Islam, is to seek to recreate Islamic society, even with its religiously imposed social prescriptions, within European society on the basis of separatism.

Indeed, any minority seeks to preserve its customs within a society with a different culture; the debate has long gone on among American Orthodox Jews and American Mormons and Amish, among others, as to how rigidly to maintain separation in daily ways of life in order to preserve culture. The basic issue is not at all necessarily the demand by Western societies for total cultural integration, absorption, and assimilation of minorities, a process legitimately feared by many minorities anxious to preserve their cultural identity. The question is, rather, whether these minorities will accept the basic tenets of Western modernism: secularism, pluralism, and tolerance.[12] These tenets are hardly unknown to Muslims, at least in principle. As noted earlier, most Middle Eastern societies are essentially secular in their legal structure and are pluralist in ethnic and/or religious makeup. Equality and tolerance for minority communities are legally stipulated, even if their application may vary sharply in practice, as in most societies where reality falls short of the ideal. But some Islamists in European societies are attempting to *avoid* integration into secular modernism in preference for separatism and even insistence on separate legal rights and procedures on family and cultural matters.

The line is a fine one. The moderate Islamist Egyptian writer Fahmi Howeidi shows anxiety toward French cultural policy that would seek to impose a "French Islam" on the 4.5 million Muslims who live in France:

> The French debate of what to do about the country's Islamic community has been under way since the Islamic phenomenon emerged in the 1970s and has become a political issue....The French parties are in full agreement on the objective—that the Moslem community must not remain a separate society with its own distinctive culture—although [the French] differ on the means. The rightists want the Moslems thrown out, but the Gaullists and Socialists want them assimilated....
>
> Assimilation, or the cultivation of a "special, domesticated" strain of Islam that conforms to the host society, is something else altogether. It is aimed at "fragmentation and secession" from Islam and is meant to sap the faith of its "true content," "gradually uprooting it." And that is the challenge

facing the Moslems of France today....

It is not a new challenge. Moslems have suffered Western "tyranny and persecution" down the ages, for ideological reasons (the Vatican, for instance, still doesn't recognize Islam as a faith), or for "civilizational reasons" (western civilization is dominant and by its nature rejects "the Other")....The massacre of the Bosnian Moslems is only the latest episode. Remember the "Morisco" Moslems of Andalusia.[13]

Yet elements of ghetto-Islam do appear in European society, especially in those areas that touch on social issues, religion, education, and sexual mores. The Muslim Institute in England, which represents a more separatist trend within the local Muslim population that is not representative of majority Muslim opinion, in 1990 issued a "Muslim Manifesto—a Strategy for Survival" that "implicitly describes Muslims in Britain as a threatened species," stating that Muslims are an autonomous community, capable of setting [their]own goals and priorities in domestic and foreign relationships." These goals include "new legal status for Islam in Britain, an extension of the [currently existing British] law on blasphemy, Islamic proselytism in Britain, Islamic schools, and the possibility of an Islamic University."[14]

British Muslims from Commonwealth states have the right to vote in the United Kingdom. Most of the Muslim population in France, some 2.5–3.0 million, cannot vote unless native-born, but the Union Islamique en France has asked for segregated male-female education; problems have developed over a desire by Muslim students to wear head scarves in class. Hardly any of Germany's 1.9 million mostly Turkish Muslims have citizenship.[15] Because of the relative degree of Westernization and secularization of Turkey, the Turkish population in Germany struggles less for separatist status of any kind but is not accepted socially in German society either.

Further problems arise with Muslims asking for special rights for Islamically sanctioned meat (the Islamic equivalent of kosher) in factories and educational institutions, time for daily prayers, and major Muslim holidays—all of which can be disruptive of Western industrial norms. Additional problems emerge over the content of moral education, the treatment of teenagers, marriage and divorce laws, and so on. Whereas some kinds of considerations can be made for Muslim culture, the European state faces problems with demands for any kind of special legal treatment beyond the laws of the state. In effect, the state cannot compromise its secular character in confrontation with these typical dilemmas of multiculturalism, dilemmas that Europe is perhaps less well equipped to cope with than is the United States.

The problem is especially compounded when coupled with terrorist incidents such as the bombing of the World Trade Center in New York in 1993, an event that evoked harsh sentiments:

> Yet one cannot deny that there is also an Arab culture in Brooklyn and Jersey City and Detroit off which the criminals feed and which gets a grim thrill from them. Ours is not a country with which they identify or whose values they share. The American flag has been a flag of convenience for them, the flag of a patsy country that lets them in without scrutiny, lets them work, go to school, organize, harangue, hate, and then, foolishly, tries to fit them into some fanciful mosaic of gorgeous diversity. It's hard to understand why they come here.[16]

Muslims are not without recognition that the problem is complex and not totally one-sided. One Middle Eastern journalist writes:

> Immigrant communities themselves need to show more understanding of their hosts' fears. Europeans have justified concerns about the effect of immigration on unemployment, and it must be acknowledged that many expatriates from Arab and Islamic countries have abused the host states' social security provisions and political asylum laws. There are also some grounds for fearing that the religious extremism that is rampant in the Middle East is taking root among expatriate communities in Europe.

But, he continues,

> the danger is that negative stereotypes of Arabs and Moslems are being promoted not just by right-wing fanatics, but by "respectable" politicians in Britain and France seeking to make political gains by stirring up xenophobia. . . . The debate about immigration in Europe is taking on an overtly racist character. Arabs and Moslems are being portrayed as innately undesirable and threatening.[17]

Recognition of this problem is spurring scholars and communities, especially in the United States, new efforts to find answers. Particularly after the World Trade Center bombing, a split has emerged between the more mainstream Islamist movement dominated by the "mainstream Islamist" Muslim Brotherhood and the more radical and violent movements or *jihadist* trend. Mainstream American Muslims themselves seek to "naturalize Islam" in the

United States. The American Moslem Council in Washington has a major mission "to get American Moslems involved in the political system and organize them into a powerful lobby capable of gaining Moslem rights under the American Constitution."[18] A group of Islamic scholars is working in Los Angeles on "minority jurisprudence," "an interpretation of the Islamic texts that would allow Moslems to make some religious concessions to meet American culture halfway."[19]

In short, major adjustments may be underway in the character of Muslim societies abroad. These developments may have considerable impact on the evolution of Islamic religious and political thinking in the Middle East as a result, for the same questions are being raised there, even in the Muslim cultural context. Just what are the implications of secular government in the Middle East? And how can law be devised that protects the rights of non-Muslims within society even where the culture is dominantly Islamic? Both radical and moderate visions of Islam are expressed by Muslims in the West, perhaps the only place in the world where there is no limitation on their political expression.

More significantly, Muslims in the West and the Middle East are beginning to grasp the importance of secular protection of their religious rights and political beliefs in the West—in sharp contrast to Middle Eastern societies, where many Muslims have died for their beliefs at the hands of the state. In effect the benefits and protection afforded to Muslims by secularism in the West may now be seen to have some relevance to the concerns of religious minorities in the Middle East, who, for their own protection, prefer to live in a secular society. New ground is thus being broken in Islamic thinking that will have major repercussions for decades to come as Muslims living in Western societies elaborate new concepts, formulate and publish their thinking, and return to their own countries. The West has now become one of the primary laboratories for rapid, virtually "forced" Islamic evolution.

The issue is also a two-way street. European and U.S. Muslim communities are also subject to influences from abroad. Large quantities of literature and tapes on Islamic subjects are sent to the West from the Middle East, and Muslim clerics and Islamist leaders travel to Muslim communities abroad. Contemporary technology makes available extraordinary new lines of communication between the two regions. Which community exerts the greater influence over the other? Do ties with the Middle East hinder the cultural assimilation of Muslims into Western society (Euro-Islam)? Or do they enable Western Muslims to turn around and export even greater influence of new ideas back to the home culture?

This question can never be decisively answered, yet much anecdotal evidence suggests that Muslims visiting the United States, at least, are regularly "set straight" by American Muslims on issues relating to Western and American society and its practices that are poorly understood in the Middle East itself. Visiting representatives of Middle Eastern states are often criticized for their own lack of liberalization in political or social terms. Indeed, Muslims in the United States are far more broadly able to meet, consult, discuss, and dispute than are their Middle Eastern counterparts. They are exposed to a far broader international community of Muslims and live in a highly liberal environment that is bound to affect at least the spirit of their inquiry and discourse. Thus, a small minority of radical Muslims in the United States—and an even smaller violent fringe—might be susceptible to thinking and directives from the Middle East, but the vast majority of the population is not so susceptible; indeed, it views its own interests in the broadest sense as separate from those of current Middle Eastern regimes or even indigenous political movements.[20]

Yet some, such as the British writer Anthony Hartley, suggest that Muslim communities "appear not to be taking the path of integration trodden by other types of immigrants. Their Islamic identity carries with it beliefs and practices that separate them from their adopted societies." This view may be more typical of the European experience than the American. European societies are generally more inclined to protect their own centuries-old local cultures and are less familiar with the broad process of assimilation and integration than is the United States, where typically assimilation takes on definable patterns over the generations, regardless of differing national origins.

There are an estimated 3 to 4 million Muslims in the United States,[21] of whom approximately one-third are African American, the rest first-generation immigrants or their children.[22] The concerns of recent immigrants resemble those of earlier European immigrants to a considerable extent, including "family values," safety in the streets, drugs, and sexual mores. Otherwise American Muslims state their firm desire to integrate into mainstream America in all respects. They are members of both political parties, but they are often Republican because they stress conservative values. Some 165 private Muslim schools exist in the United States, but 90 percent of Muslim children go to public school. Many Muslims manage to take off the necessary five minutes or so for brief prayer during the work day with no problems at work. In addition to prayer time, goals of the Muslim community include a call for "school textbooks free of anti-Islamic stereotypes, permission at school and work to observe Muslim holidays, Muslim chaplains in the armed forces, the availability of food that meets Islam's dietary code, a drug-free, less sexually permissive environment for their children."[23]

American and European Muslims are affected by deep anxiety during terrorist incidents committed against the West by Muslims anywhere, especially in the United States, and by situations such as Iran's hostage taking of Americans in 1979 and the Gulf War confrontation. Under these circumstances communities are likely to develop strong mainstream pressures against radical elements within the community. "Are there kooks among the Muslims? Of course there are, and we should be entitled to have our share of zealots and kooks," as one American Muslim leader put it.[24] But lasting cultural stereotypes in the West—in part due to the relatively recent arrival of the bulk of Muslim immigrants, within the last two decades—remain a problem that complicates Muslim relations within host countries, especially during violent crises wherever they may be. Over the long run, however, assimilation into American society seems relatively straightforward and within the general context of the American assimilation of immigrants—a process perhaps less smooth in the European context and experience.

Muslim communities in the West are more likely to exert influence on their countries and cultures of origin than to receive influences from them; over time they may have a substantive effect on the perception of secularization and minority rights in the Middle East itself. The presence of Islam in the West, therefore, has powerful implications for the long-term relationship between Islam and the West—a process that is just getting under way.

Notes

1. One possible exception is Kuwait in the 1990s, which suffered the direct brunt of Iraq's invasion, pillaging, and annexation of the Kuwaiti state, as a result of which nearly all elements of the population now welcome a Western commitment to their future defense.

2. R. K. Ramazani, *Revolutionary Iran* (Baltimore: Johns Hopkins University Press, 1988), p. 123.

3. Ibid., p. 124.

4. It should be noted, however, that after the Islamists came to power in Sudan in 1989, they inaugurated quite stringent economic policies to meet a desperate, inherited economic crisis. They were willing to conform to IMF strictures in many respects, until broader ideological problems and

continuing economic problems and Sudanese nonpayment of debts finally brought about a break with the IMF.

5. Fahmi Howeidi in Egypt's *Al-Ahram,* quoted in *Mideast Mirror,* September 21, 1993, p. 20.

6. Ahmad Jum'aa in Bahrain's *Al-Ayyam,* quoted in *Mideast Mirror,* January 24, 1994, pp. 13–14.

7. Ahmad Nafei in Egypt's *Al-Ahram,* quoted in *Mideast Mirror,* April 13, 1994, p. 12.

8. The author has heard accounts of this problem repeatedly from a wide variety of Muslim parents who have emigrated to the United States from a variety of Muslim countries—Iran, Pakistan, the Arab world, and Turkey—and who are attempting to preserve some semblance of more conservative values with their second-generation teenagers, only with considerable difficulty.

9. In traditional Muslim states before the modern period, Shari'a law stipulates the extension of broad legal rights and protections to non-Muslim religious communities, but not on a basis of full equality for participation in government. Nor had a large Muslim community enjoyed legal equality or even protection in other non-Muslim states before. See Wilfred Cantwell Smith, *Islam in Modern History,* (Princeton, NJ: University Press, 1957), p. 267, pp. 286–287.

10. Indeed, the problem of Muslims in India today is that they face a powerful and growing Hindu fundamentalist movement that seeks to reverse India's secular character in favor of an official Hindu character.

For an excellent discussion of the Muslim dilemma in India, see Saeed Naqvi, *Reflections of an Indian Muslim* (New Delhi: Har-Anand Publications, 1993).

11. These terms are used by Bassam Tibi in "Bedroht uns der Islam?" (Does Islam Threaten Us?), *Der Spiegel,* No. 5, 1993, p. 127.

12. Ibid., p. 127.

13. See Fahmi Howeidi in *Al-Sharq al-Awsat,* as quoted in the *Middle East Mirror,* March 22, 1993, p. 21.

14. Anthony Hartley, "Europe's Muslims," *The National Interest,* Winter 1990/91, p. 57.

15. Ibid., pp. 59–60.

16. "The Immigrants," *New Republic,* April 19, 1993, p. 7, is a classic example of that publication's characteristic anti-Muslim animus.

17. Raghib al-Solh in the pan-Arab *al-Hayat,* as quoted in the *Middle East Mirror,* June 4, 1993, p. 14.

18. Jamal Khashoggi in *al-Hayat,* as quoted in the *Middle East Mirror,* March 26, 1993, p. 18.

19. Ibid.

20. The author (Graham E. Fuller) has formed many of these views in the course of frequent discussions over the years with American Muslims, especially second-generation.

21. There are no official statistics, since the Department of Immigration does not keep track of immigrants' religious faith.

22. See Richard Bernstein, "A Growing Islamic Presence: Balancing Sacred and Secular" (a four-part series on Islam in the United States), *New York Times,* May 2, 1993.

23. *New York Times,* May 7, 1993.

24. Ibid.

6

THE RELIGIOUS DIMENSION

How much is Islam itself a factor in the frictions that currently exist between the Muslim world and the non-Muslim or Western world? Scholars and pundits have spent much time examining Islam to determine whether or not its theology predetermines a clash with the non-Islamic world. Similarly, debate rages over whether Islam is compatible with democracy or even progress. This chapter looks at the theological question and attempts to determine the place of Islamic theology, if any, in the relationship between Islam and the West and the integration of Islamist parties into the modern political order.

In essence this analysis concludes that Islam as a theology is not the real issue. The true issue is about the kinds of interpretation given to Islam by Muslims. Not surprisingly, Muslims across a broad political spectrum use Islam to serve their own political ends—as religion is often used in other societies. Nonetheless, the structure and historic development of Islamic theology and law does predispose Islam to focus less on individual rights and more on individual obligations and the creation of the "just society" as a whole. This reality presents Islam with new tasks of interpretation to extend Islamic law to bring it into conformity with the major features of contemporary Western international law.

In the end the future of Islamic law in the contemporary legal order, especially the international legal order, can take one of three directions: The first possibility is that Islam can bring about reform within itself through already existing mechanisms. The necessary foundations exist in the Quran, the Hadith (body of historical records about the Prophet's rulings and practices) that could, in principle, justify numerous contemporary, more flexible interpretations. Two devices within Islam are available for this process of further reform: reinterpretation or extension of earlier legal precedents *(ijtihad)* and revision by consensus of Islamic scholars or even the sense of the community *(ijma')*.[1]

This will happen only if Muslim scholars or the Muslim community at large wishes it to happen, enabling reformist views to replace those of the more literalist or radical interpreters who dominate the Islamist political scene today. Regrettably, this will not be easily accomplished, since the current psychological and political dynamic within Islamic societies immensely complicates the task. The reality is that the contemporary Muslim community, in most countries under pressure or crisis from international forces as well as domestic despotism and deteriorating social and economic conditions, is drawn more toward the stark reductionism of the Islamists than toward the more open, more "Westernized" versions of Islam. People do not usually turn to liberal, less familiar forms of belief or to the spirit of experimentation with deep cultural traditions and values in times of crisis. On the contrary, they are inclined to revert to familiar basics in values and traditions. When contemporary Islamic society is seen as failing, the Islamists argue that it is precisely the departure from the fundamentals of Islam that lies at the root of the problem.

The dynamics of politics also reinforces this tendency. The harder-line Muslims have seized the initiative with a clear-cut call; through their commitment to radical action they are galvanizing battered publics. It is difficult to imagine a more moderate interpretation of Islam, one that tends to vitiate the starker interpretations of the past ("well, maybe Islam does permit alcohol as long as it is not in excess") as capable of recapturing the political initiative from the Islamists whose strength lies in the appeal to cultural authenticity. Indeed, if one's predilections are for a more reformed Islam, one would probably not vote for a moderate Islamist position but would, rather, be drawn to a more liberal political party in which Islam did not figure prominently in the political platform.

In short, we are talking about a fundamental struggle within Islam itself. If successful, a reform process would satisfy the Muslim preference for "authenticity" in society: An Islamic basis and justification would exist for conformity with modern international practice without having to go outside the tradition and borrow wholesale from a Western corpus of law. But the reality is that the political spectrum of Islamist politics under current conditions is not hospitable to strong reformist tendencies within Islam, even though such tendencies and intellectual foundations clearly exist. The future of a strong Islamic reform movement, dedicated to building an Islamic basis for construction of a modern body of Islamic law in conformity with most Western and international norms, is therefore not bright.

The second possibility is that Islam will not undergo the interpretive process necessary to make it fully compatible with existing international law. Islamic law will thus remain relegated to increasingly narrower areas of life while supplemental law is adopted from Western systems. In effect there would be a dual-level system of law, one Islamic and the other Western, covering different areas of human life, but the former area continually shrinking. This pattern is already well under way in most Muslim countries.

The third possibility is that the Islamist vision will be rejected by the majority of Muslims, and no other modernist Islamic vision will replace it. Islam will, in short, completely fail to make the transition to modernization and reform that would allow it, and not imported legal structures, to be the foundation of a modern legal system. Under these circumstances Islam will become virtually irrelevant to practical civic life in the Middle East and elsewhere, will drop out of any formal legal role, and instead will be relegated almost completely to the area of private values and private belief. Islamic holidays would remain, and Islamic traditions would remain in much of the cultural and social life, but society and the state would become formally secular. This model already exists in Turkey.

The Theological Problem

The two most active universalist world faiths are Christianity and Islam. Political and territorial rivalry has intermittently existed between them for as long as religion has been the defining ideological coinage of international struggle. Are there theological grounds that could predispose Islam to a confrontation with the non-Islamic world? Yes, in purely theological terms it is possible to find in Islam some theoretical groundwork by which to justify a state of permanent tension with the non-Muslim world if that is the goal.

The concept of *jihad* (holy struggle) invariably attracts the attention of those who posit Islam's theological hostility against the West. Critics point out that in Islamic terms the world is divided into *Dar al-Islam* (The Realm of Islam) and *Dar al-Harb* (The Realm of War), that is, into the realm of Islamic territory and a realm of permanent ongoing contention between Islam and non-Islam. In crude Cold War terms this view was attributed to a theoretically expansionist communist camp: "What is mine is mine and what is yours is subject to negotiation." In Islam *jihad* suggests a standing religious obligation upon Muslims to permanent struggle for the expansion of the Faith, a position still taken by some radical Islamists today.[2] Thus, in purely theological terms, justification for these views can be found.[3]

But we must be very careful to avoid confusing elements of religious doctrine with the realities of life. Radicals will always exist in any society, and to justify their beliefs those radicals will turn to the highest "laws" of life and society—either to God, race, or the supposedly inexorable forces of history. Most religious movements possess uncompromising zealots who insist on total and literal acceptance of all articles of faith and harsh treatment of those who fail to observe these precepts. The problem for the West, therefore, lies not specifically in Islam but in the radical visions of all extremists within any such movement. Within Islam the problem resides with those who possess a strong, activist anti-Western agenda. Many are particularly hostile to the West because they perceive Western culture to be powerful, threatening, and intrusive upon nativist visions, cultures, and interests—but that objection is *political and cultural* in nature rather than theological.

Then what is *jihad* in the modern context? Whereas radical and visionary leaders might theoretically seek the continuing expansion of Islam throughout the world, in fact the most urgent goal for nearly all Islamist clerics is to preserve and purify Islam within the existing Muslim world. In reality Islam has witnessed only minor expansion since the colonial period began.[4] In this sense Islam is no longer a "faith on the march," acquiring new realms and territories as it did in its classic periods of expansion. It is thus the internal focus of the Islamists that is one of their most distinctive features: In fact, the *jihad* today is almost exclusively *within* Islam, not at its borderlands where *jihad* has classically been conducted.[5] The pressing mission is to remake the very moral fiber of Islamic society, to restore to it the values that had made it strong, and to preserve a society perceived to be unraveling before the West. Whereas in the past Islam has seen many purifying and reformist movements seeking a return to the basics, the contemporary Islamist movement is distinctive in Islamic history in its internal focus and its eye on political power. *Jihad* is in reality no longer externally focused upon the victory of Islam in non-Muslim regions.[6]

Any revolutionary vision of Islam in the world also seems far from the minds of the majority of clerics at such mainstays of Sunni Islamic faith as the authoritative and establishment al-Azhar University in Cairo, where there is no call for *jihad,* against the West or against Christianity. Even in Shi'ite Islam, which is more revolutionary in character, many Shi'ite religious clerics opposed to the Khomeini regime in Iran or living outside Iran take sharp issue with Khomeini's own theology that proclaims a theocracy or some kind of preordained religious struggle with the West. In short, today it is difficult to find active support for ideas of permanent struggle between Islam and the West in most circles of Islam, radical or conventional.

At least as important as the influence of the radicals and the clergy is the popular perception of Islam and the West. Few Muslims in their daily lives and in interaction with Westerners nourish any kind of concept of implacable hostility or the need for confrontation. The West is a daily reality in the lives of nearly all Muslims; it is a culture many of whose features Muslims admire: education, technology, concepts of liberty, respect for human rights, rule of law, and improved standards of living. Muslims know they must come to terms with this Western reality, and in fact they do so without hesitation; it surrounds them from birth. Muslims travel regularly and extensively to the West, marry Westerners, receive education in the West, and reside there for long periods of time.

Yet acceptance of the Western presence in the world does not exclude strong opposition to the West when a perception exists that Muslims are suffering from explicit Western policies and actions. Oppression and humiliation of Muslims, violence against them, or perceived disregard of Muslim vital interests on the part of Western powers will regularly spark a hostile response. Extremists seek to strengthen that hostile response by casting it in the most exalted terms possible: religious terms.

In effect, it is not religion that is evoking radical behavior but specific conditions that are evoking radical responses couched in religious terms. As the level of Islamic rhetoric rises, the more it facilitates the adoption of a sense of grievance and the search for blame. A vicious circle is thus easily formed. Indeed, history shows how readily radical responses to conditions can also be couched in terms of various other "higher forces" such as tribalism, nationalism, or class struggle. In short, these radical responses to problems in the political, social, and economic environment will emerge under almost any circumstances and will invariably seek some form of dramatic and legitimizing public formulation. For many decades in many parts of the world, that formulation of protest was communism. In short, the grievances are there and will not go away, whether Islam is the specific vehicle or not.

As do the holy writings in any religion, the Quran and the Hadith provide a rich source of ideas that can be used to justify a multitude of views, even contradictory ones. In Latin America Roman Catholic worker-priests with leftist social agendas, faced with overwhelming social problems, have also expressed their struggle in religious and theological terms, even if ultimately disavowed by the Catholic Church. Islam becomes "dangerous" to the extent that it can provide framework and justification for radicalism that can be directed against the West as well as against local regimes. Modern Islamism, in particular, has been particularly adept at translating existing serious grievances into Islamic terms and creating the social movement and local institutions whereby these grievances become actionable. But ideas are also found within Islam that council moderation, prudence, tolerance, and reconciliation, and these are used by many Muslim authorities to combat Islamic radicalism. Again, the struggle is not between Islam and non-Islam but among ideas and movements within Islamic culture as a whole.

Of course, some Islamic political movements, or fringes of political movements, do exist that can clearly be described as dangerous. They are dangerous because they espouse and often commit violent action, frequently in locales where conditions are already volatile. The problem here is not that the ideas and vocabulary of the movement are Islamic, but that their expression is criminal, including assassinations and bombings. Such criminal actions require a firm response, by force where necessary, as well as legal action. The potentially fatal mistake committed by so many besieged Muslim governments such as in Algeria, Egypt, and Tunisia is to confuse the message with the action. These regimes often fail to differentiate among the various aspects of political Islam. Lumping all Islamic groups together in a wave of condemnation regardless of their views or means of operation risks placing established regimes in the unenviable position of seeming to war against Islam itself—a potentially fatal perception.

The other fateful alternative often chosen by embattled regimes is to attempt to "out-Islam" the Islamists in a competition to prove how committed to Islam the regimes themselves are. Leaders will start invoking the Qumran regularly in their speeches, are photographed regularly at prayer, will take the lead in banning certain kinds of films, books, and foreign television programs, even banning alcohol in certain venues, and speaking out in favor of aspects of the Islamist agenda. By adopting so many of the trappings of Islam, regimes combating the Islamists have in a way allowed the Islamists to set the entire framework of debate—in purely Islamic terms.

Existing governments are unlikely to succeed in proving that they are "more Islamic" than the Islamist opposition because in fact Islam is not the issue at all. Governments are under siege from the Islamists mainly because most of them are open to charges of incompetence, corruption, authoritarianism, or the arbitrary use of force by the security services. When governments attempt to prove Islamic credentials without changing the status quo, the credentials become largely meaningless, and attempts to invoke them only strengthen the Islamist position. Standing governments everywhere also labor under the disadvantage of having to cope with highly complex economic and social problems in which success is hard to come by. Even under the best of circumstances they are not likely to meet the abstract and theoretical standards called for by Islamist movements that have never had either power or responsibility and hence never had to compromise their own principles with the reality of running a country.

As a result, the Egyptian government, for example, has shifted the debate onto the Islamists' own terms. The regime is trying to prove its Islamic credentials in all areas, thereby abandoning any pretense of support for secular or liberal values. At the same time this kind of debate has caused even mainstream clerics to escalate their own level of rhetoric whereby even major figures in establishment Islam are now vying with the Islamists in the field of intolerance. This polarized situation permits many narrow and non-liberal clerics within Islam to pass for mainstream. In one of the most egregious examples, Shaykh Muhammad al-Ghozali, of the distinguished al-Azhar School of Theology and a frequent government spokesman on Islam on Egyptian television, stated in an interview that "a secularist represents a danger to society and the nation [and] must be eliminated. . . . It is the duty of the Government to kill him."[7]

Although many variations and interpretations about the meaning of the Quran and Islamic law are possible, the Islamists have managed to establish a near monopoly based on radical and narrow interpretations in most cases. This interpretation is resented by many Muslims who see this as an infringement upon their own rights and a denial of alternative interpretations of how Islam is to be observed. Algerian demonstrators against the radical Islamists have carried banners proclaiming, "It is not your Islam, it is our Islam." This is precisely the issue: Whose Islam is it? Unfortunately, there is no national debate over whose Islam it is, although the Egyptian government has undertaken information campaigns to convince the public of the errors of Islamist tactics and theology, including feature-length dramas for television and the cinema about innocent Egyptian youth recruited into radical Islam. Radical groups have in effect preempted Islam for themselves, yet in a volatile social environment no other elements from within Islam seem willing to seriously contest the issue in ways effective among the broader public.

In principle one possible source of disagreement about whose Islam it is could come from the traditional Islamic establishment and clergy. But establishment Islam is largely captive to the state and working to serve the needs of the state, thereby lacking legitimacy. Establishment Islam that does not itself undertake criticism of the shortcomings of existing regimes thus loses all credibility in the eyes of the public and is taken to be in the regime's pocket, even sometimes chillingly referred to by the Islamists as *al-Islam al-Amriki*, "American Islam." Only a religious establishment independent enough to serve as loyal opposition to the state might be able to retain sufficient credibility with the public to deprive the Islamists of their monopoly of opposition.

There is no doubt, then, that Islam as a theology can be used as a powerful political weapon by radical Islamist groups against the externally chosen enemy—now the West, but in the past the Soviet Union as well—and against the internal enemy, that is, the regime in power. Like all great world religions Islam reaches for transcendent ideals and for the perfection of society in accordance with God's law. The gulf between the reality of human society and government, on the one hand, and the ideals of religion, on the other, will always be pronounced. The gulf can always be used to justify attacks against the state or against those external forces perceived to hamper attainment of a God-ordained society on earth. The appeal to religion will take on greater force and resonance the more the public perceives a deterioration of its own circumstances.

This phenomenon is not unique to Islam. Certainly Christian groups have used their faith over the centuries to criticize social conditions and unjust regimes. Hinduism today has adopted many militant stands on the need to desecularize Indian society, as have militant Buddhist movements in Sri Lanka in struggling against Hinduism, and the Sikh faith in India against Hinduism.[8] Religion is increasingly used as a political instrument and as a rallying cry in unstable societies and conditions. Although Islam is not alone in this phenomenon, there are features of Islam that lend themselves to such political usage. Semitic religions in general, and Islam in particular, tend to be highly specific about the concrete details of society and governance in the religiously sanctioned life. Thus extensive and detailed rules about a broad body of personal, family, and social conduct exist, and these can be cited when the state or society is perceived to be violating them. This detailed body of specific religious law or practice, even if no longer observed by many Muslim states (e.g., the ban on alcohol) tends to facilitate the use of Islam toward political and social ends.

In sum, then, Islam as a faith is not the problem. The battle is over the uses of Islam. The challenge is to develop tactics by which extremist or fringe religious elements can legally be politically sidelined without violence or repression.

Notes

1. Bernard Lewis, *The Political Language of Islam* (Chicago: Chicago University Press, 1988), p. 29. For a discussion of this process in contemporary Islamist thinking, also see G. H. Jansen, *Militant Islam* (London: Pan Books, 1979), pp. 24–25.

2. For that matter, many religions maintain the concept of militant commitment to the propagation of the faith and its values—witness the hallowed Christian hymn "Onward Christian Soldiers, marching as to war, with the Cross of Jesus, going on before."

In Israel significant fundamentalist movements exist led by past and present leaders such as Rabbi Avraham Yitzhak Kuk, Rabbi Meir Kahane, Gershon Salomon (Faithful of the Temple Mount); "they believe that the establishment of a truly Jewish state is not only a symbolic religious act but also a crucial step toward the redemption of the entire cosmos. . . . they are convinced that they have the ability to change the course of history." According to a body of theory propagated by Kahane, the moment of divine redemption will come with the "re-creation of the biblical state of Israel. . . . Israel should be ruled strictly according to Jewish law; non-Jews—for that matter even secular Jews—had no place in this sacred order." See Juergensmeyer, *The New Cold War?* pp. 65–69.

3. See, for example, the discussion in Lewis, *The Political Language of Islam.*

4. Major exceptions are in sub-Saharan Africa, among African Americans, and perhaps to a modest degree in Western Europe and India (refugees from the caste system), and greater presence in the West primarily due to immigration.

5. Ali El-Kenz, *Algerian Reflections on Arab Crises* (Austin: Center for Middle Eastern Studies, Texas University Press, 1991), p. 95.

6. One small exception is in sub-Saharan Africa, where some Islamists feel there is room for propagation of the faith, especially among animists. This missionary work is still marginal within the broader confines of Islamic activism, but it worries African governments.

7. Youssef Ibrahim. "Egypt Fights Militant Islam with More of the Same," *New York Times,* August 18, 1993.

8. Juergensmeyer, *The New Cold War?* pp. 81–109.

7

SOLIDARITY AND COEXISTENCE

The task for Western and Muslim societies and states is to learn how to coexist at a time of rapid change in a world in which relationships forged during the Cold War era are rapidly giving way to a more fluid and unstable world, with new aspirations for Third World peoples. This chapter examines the character of Muslim aspirations for solidarity, what they mean for the West, and the kinds of internal changes necessary in the political systems of the Muslim world before Muslim states can alter chronic patterns of instability that unsettle relations with the West. In short, how can the West and the Muslim world coexist in this period of potentially serious turmoil?

Islamic Solidarity—How Likely?

First, most Muslims view solidarity among Muslim states as desirable, at least in principle. This view is entirely natural. Realistically speaking, to what extent might Islam provide the cohesiveness to permit Muslim countries as a group to achieve a new degree of solidarity among themselves? And to what extent would that solidarity be especially directed against the West? In simplest terms, Islam per se cannot accomplish solidarity among Muslim states if the practical wherewithal for solidarity is otherwise missing. Does a sufficiently broad set of common grievances and goals exist among Muslim states or populations to enable Muslims to coalesce and establish a voice under the banner of Islam? Second, is the West necessarily the major source of those grievances or merely a contributing force?

These questions must concern the West if it is to avoid facile talk of broader or inevitable "civilizational conflict." Once sensitized to the nature of Muslim grievances, the West can choose (or not) to ameliorate or eliminate those sources of grievance where possible. Where grievances are mutual dialogue can obviously facilitate some compromise. Where fundamental clashes of interests exist, the political cost of permitting those clashes to persist must be assessed. The greater the scope and depth of grievances, the greater the likelihood of their consolidation into some broader brief against the West as a whole, rather than remaining as a set of distinct and separate problems. Unless things go wrong in the Middle East and Western policies are extremely short-sighted, there is no reason to believe that Muslim grievances should rise to the level of civilizational clash. If they do attain such dramatic form, then the outlook will be very serious indeed for both sides.

Let us examine the factors that will contribute to Muslim solidarity and those factors that militate against it. Solidarity can be enhanced by negative or positive stimuli. Among Muslim states solidarity has generally been most enhanced by negative factors, or common grievances, especially against common enemies. However, positive factors such as a keen desire to pursue common values could also play a role. Islamists speak of common values but have not yet developed a clear-cut, concrete body of positive programs and approaches that most of the Muslim world can agree on. The Islamist agenda, furthermore, remains mired in what are largely negative issues at this phase of its development—excessive focus on identification of things that are illicit, improper, and should be banned, and far less emphasis on concrete positive goals.

Key Preconditions for Islamic Solidarity

What are the preconditions for a consolidated Muslim front against the West? Although the range of issues and grievances is broad, as discussed in Chapter 3, basically only three categories of catalyst exist: deep domestic discontent, major international events in which Muslims are perceived as victims of Western action, and the attainment of power by radical Islamist movements.

Domestic discontent in the Muslim world is the single most important prerequisite for the international growth of radical Islamist forces. When popular discontent with local conditions is at manageable levels, then international issues in and of themselves are not likely to rally major radical Islamist movements across international borders. Unfortunately, domestic discontent is prevalent in numerous Muslim countries: Deepening economic problems, unemployment and lack of opportunity, high population growth rates with which governments cannot keep pace in providing social services and infrastructure, poorly administered and inefficient state sectors, corruption, poor government, absence of representative government all feature among the key grievances. Most regimes in the region suffer from a crisis of legitimacy because they are not elected and often have little basis for genuine legitimacy in time of crisis.

Domestic discontent often translates into a growth of radicalism. As long as unfavorable domestic conditions exist at insupportable levels, Western policies designed to lessen radicalism in the Muslim world will be largely ineffectual. Unfortunately, for at least a decade, Islamist movements have provided virtually the only alternative political vehicle to oppose failing, corrupt, or unrepresentative regimes and policies. Few other vibrant opposition movements exist at the moment, in part because of deliberate government policies designed to weaken, neutralize, or even eliminate all opposition. In short, Islamist movements have now become the single most likely successors to failed regimes.

The West is not, of course, directly at fault for ineffective governance in Muslim states. Nonetheless, Western policies have partially contributed to failed governance by lending support to authoritarian regimes and by a strong preference for stability over change across the Middle East. This perception is especially acute when failing governments are closely allied with the West. Such accumulated public anger can readily be turned against the West when coupled with dramatic developments on the international scene.

The second potential catalyst for Muslim consolidation emerges from foreign policy crises that produce severe setbacks, humiliation, or suffering to Muslims. Traditional Muslim issues have consistently included the Palestinians' unresolved grievances, Western military attacks against Muslim states, and most recently the Bosnian crisis. Because the Bosnian Muslims are broadly perceived as the chief victims in the broader Yugoslav crisis and because the West is seen as having done little to improve their position, the Muslim world perceives such inaction as tantamount to a Western desire to eliminate one of the last centers of Muslim population and culture on Western soil. For a long time to come the Bosnian question will remain a running sore and symbol of anti-Muslim religious oppression in the West. It is becoming the "new Palestinian issue" in terms of its emotionalism and symbolic significance to Muslims everywhere—precisely because it is in Europe. Unless dramatically and justly resolved from the Muslim point of view, the Bosnian issue will complicate Western diplomatic intervention elsewhere in the Muslim world for the indefinite future.

Western military intervention in the Muslim world in general will grow more costly in years ahead as the Muslim world develops new expectations regarding international prestige and equality. These attitudes are exemplified by rising feelings among most of the Third World and non-European peoples everywhere. A typical example is the reaction to the U.S. cruise missile attack on Iraqi intelligence headquarters in June 1993 in response to an Iraqi plot to assassinate ex-President Bush. Whatever the case against Saddam Hussein, the action met with a cold response even from Middle East allies. An analysis of Middle East press commentary concluded:

> Reaction ranges from varying degrees of embarrassed silence among most of Washington's Arab allies, to disgusted outrage at what is perceived as a cynical and unjustified attack. . . . The overriding feeling in the Arab world is one of anger and humiliation at the self-styled guardian of the new world order's apparent disregard for international law as it pursues its vendetta against its favorite Arab bogey-man with scant regard for the innocent civilians it kills in the process.[1]

The West's assaults against Arab leaders—even unpopular leaders such as Qadhafi—are viewed as uncalled-for Western arrogation of privilege to discipline the Arab world. Whereas no single event in isolation is likely to spark revolution, the accumulated sense of grievance serves to develop dangerous tendencies of alienation, which can gradually accumulate in people who move into positions of responsibility and authority—even in Middle Eastern military establishments—and create unexpected reservoirs of support for Islamist expression that can emerge suddenly at critical political junctures. Large numbers of responsible and Westernized Muslims inwardly exult at Western policy failures or at ripostes to the West by unpalatable dictators. Although these Muslims themselves might never articulate such views, the feelings lurk beneath the surface as a secret pleasure at an overdue comeuppance to Western power. Thus, international incidents affecting the fate of Muslims at the hands of the West will serve, more than anything else, to crystallize local discontent and channel it in the form of Muslim solidarity against the West.

Third, the future emergence of one or more radical Islamist regimes in the Muslim world can also serve as a regional catalyst to a more consolidated Islamic stance vis-à-vis the West. Not all members of the public support Islamist policies, of course, but several Islamist victories can create a bandwagon effect of irresistibility that will greatly strengthen other Islamist movements in the region. As long as volatile conditions exist in the region, either domestically or internationally, radical forces are in a position to exploit them. Radical Arab nationalist regimes have done so in the past. Today Islamist regimes are also likely to identify existing problems within Muslim societies as possessing roots in Western colonialism or in current Western policies. Islamist movements will not be new or unique in exploiting accumulated grievances against the West, but they could be quite effective.

Therefore, these basic preconditions strengthen Islamic solidarity and contribute to the strength of Islamist movements in an international setting. Additional specific issues could contribute to increased feelings of Islamic solidarity.

- Perceived "cultural aggression," such as the publication of Salman Rushdie's *Satanic Verses.* This issue would not have become such a *cause célèbre* had it not been trumpeted by Iran well after publication and criticism elsewhere, leading to an Iranian bounty on Rushdie's head, and thus producing Western countermoves against Iran in the name of freedom of speech. This classic culture war, with no winners, polarized the issue: The West seemed to champion the cause of blasphemy, with Muslims championing intellectual terrorism.
- Restrictive European immigration policies that seem to discriminate against Muslims, their ability to work in Europe, and their freedom to send remittances to their home countries.
- Social discrimination against Muslims in Europe, most egregiously as the killing of Turkish guest-workers by German skinheads, but also in more subtle ways such as denying Muslim educational concerns or limiting Muslim entry into professional circles.
- Economic discrimination in which the Muslim world, especially along the borders of Europe (e.g., Turkey and the Maghreb), is excluded from new economic associations and ties in the European Community.
- A perception that the new world order is designed to allow a handful of Western states to pursue their own international agenda at the expense of the Third World in general and the Muslim world in particular.
- Western rebuff of Third World aspirations for greater power sharing on the level of international politics and organizations. The years ahead will show greater pressures for increased representation of Third World, but especially Muslim, representation in bodies such as the UN Security Council. Egypt, Pakistan, Algeria, Turkey, or Indonesia appear to be leading candidates for this position.

Factors Working Against Muslim Solidarity

Traditional Ethnic, Regional, and Sectarian Differences
The Muslim world encompasses an immense variety of peoples and cultures with vastly differing historical experiences. Genuine differences in

outlook among major ethnic groups—Arab, Turk, or Persian, for example—can work to produce suspicion or even conflict. These ethnic divisions often weigh more heavily than the unifying aspects of Islamic culture, depending on the issue. Tribalism or ethnicity has always been perceived by Muslims as a dangerous factor in Islam, standing in the way of a more universal religious community.

Rivalries exist even within the shared culture of the Arab states themselves, often based on long-standing geopolitical competition. The Nile Valley is an ancient rival to the Mesopotamian. Egypt and Syria have contended for power along the Levant coast for thousands of years. The Arabian peninsula has fought against the northern Arab regions; north and south within the Arabian peninsula itself demonstrate profound cultural and psychological differences. Modern Arab states continue to jockey for position against each other. Thus the Arab world is far from united politically, making unanimity of view difficult to attain on most issues, regardless of how critical these issues may be for the region. But in its divisiveness the Arab world is hardly alone in the world. On the contrary, in an age when separatism and centrifugal forces are tearing numerous states apart, the Arab world is one of the few regions at least displaying a constant public longing for unity. If calls for separatism are ready-made tools for political rabble-rousing in most parts of the world today, in the Arab world it is calls for unity that stir public opinion. The ideal goes beyond mere rhetoric: Many popularly received schemes for unity have been implemented among many different Arab states at different times, but nearly all of them have foundered as a result of poor conception or implementation.

Subnational ethnic differences within existing multinational and multisectarian states have also left a deep and divisive legacy. Kurds, Berbers, Azeris, Tajiks, Baluch, Pashtun, Uzbeks, Hazara, Punjabi, and Sindhis are but a few of the significant ethnic groups in the greater Middle East, groups who as minorities in one state or another have uneasy relationships with the state. Religion, too, divides: Differences between Shi'ites and Sunnis, among differing Shi'ite and Sunni sects, 'Alawites, Maronites, Druze, Copts, Ahmedis, Baha'is—all represent potential fracture lines in society. Historically, outsiders, including Western governments, have exploited and even magnified these differences, for purposes of subjugation and geopolitical advantage during the colonial era, although these differences are hardly a creation of Western policies themselves. Few Muslim states have evolved societies or polities with successful legal structures that genuinely protect minority rights or provide sufficient cultural autonomy or federal arrangements to handle sharply distinct cultural communities. Until Muslim societies develop these legal mechanisms and structures, individual states will be weak and the region will be prey to dissension that prevents strong unity of purpose.

Many Arab and Muslim scholars have accused the West of deliberately creating an entire body of literature and scholarship—encyclopedias or handbooks of problems and divisions in the region—to be used to keep Muslims divided.[2] As noted above, there is no question that these differences have been exploited in the past by outside powers, not only Western. Yet these differences and dissensions do not go away by ignoring their existence. Many Muslims cling to the notion that if good government exists, it will overcome all differences. In fact, only through recognition of these diversities, differing aspirations, and historical grievances can political structures be built to meet such problems and eventually alleviate them.

Differing Socioeconomic Bases

The divide between haves and have-nots in the Muslim world is another significant fault line that tends to hinder cooperation. Oil-rich states tend to be resented by those without oil, especially when the oil and wealth is perceived to lead citizens to display arrogance toward older and more established, if poorer, cultural centers such as Cairo or Damascus. Unequal economic relationships are likewise a source of discontent, sometimes leading to revolutionary clarion-calls, such as practiced by Gamal Abdel Nasser or Saddam Hussein. The existence of oil wealth has also served to preserve traditional ruling structures such as monarchy. Even the political style and international orientation of the oil state differs from the non-oil state: State wealth can be used to alleviate many social and political problems that in poorer states are sometimes dealt with simply by stricter security systems. Oil states are usually treated more deferentially on the international stage than states without oil or wealth; their economies too, are affected differently by changes on the world economic scene.

Differing Security Perceptions

Two factors greatly affect the security perceptions of Muslim states: ideological differences and possession of oil wealth. Fear of radical neighbors causes many oil states to prefer security ties with the West rather than trust in any inter-Arab system of collective security. During the Cold War, Turkey, Iran, and Pakistan shared anxiety about Soviet intentions and capabilities; only in the West were they able to find support to meet their security needs. The Muslim states of East Asia and Africa face quite different security problems and threats than does the Arab world. In fact, in terms of security issues Muslim states at present have little in common. They have no single neighbor to fear apart from Israel: Aggression could come from any source, depending on the evolution of politics. Each state's national security policy, then, will remain a source of divisiveness. As long as the region is hostage to unpredictable ideological states, no natural and sustained cooperation among Muslim states can be expected, especially on security issues.

In sum, differences in character, outlook, economy, and geopolitics tend to differentiate the Muslim states. It is natural that such a diversity of states, structures, peoples, cultures, and geography would create differing outlooks on the world and the conduct of foreign relations. The question is: How strong will the force of shared Islamic culture weigh against other national interests? In reality differing Muslim states will probably share more in common with some Western states, on some issues, some of the time, than they will jointly among themselves. In other words, although Islamic solidarity is an attractive ideal, the world is too complicated for that. Relationships among states will be based on a wide variety of interests and preferences, shifting over time, rather than on a single ideological principle.

How should the West think about Muslim solidarity? Solidarity in itself is a neutral quality. Political judgments about Muslim solidarity, like solidarity in any group, depend very much on the ideology driving it or the end to which it is directed. Under circumstances of marked friction between Muslim and Western states, Islamic solidarity will obviously enable Muslim states to deal from a position of strength. To the extent that Washington is broadly in conflict with the Muslim world, Muslim solidarity cannot be perceived as positive in the West. It is the solidarity of radicalism—based either on naked political power and radical political ideology or on the social despair of dysfunctional governments and societies—that provides the West with serious grounds for concern. To the extent that solidarity is based upon international norms of behavior and the development of democratic and free societies, the ability of a Muslim bloc to maintain these standards would be very positive from a Western point of view.

Only increased mutual trust, which can come only from more transparent, moderate, predictable, and democratic governance, can lead to more confident cooperation among Muslim states. If the Muslim world seeks greater unity and commonness of purpose, it will need to attend to these urgent internal problems. If dictatorship, irresponsible and unconstrained leadership, and mutual suspicions are the norm in most of the Muslim world, then real

Muslim unity is likely to be extremely limited, perhaps existing only at the "street" level in times of international crisis.

The West itself obviously has a major role to play in avoiding policies that lead to the crystallization of widespread opposition against it. Moderate, constructive, and equitable policies on the part of the West toward the Muslim world will be a strong factor serving to limit the prospects of a hostile Muslim coalition uniting against the West.

The Islamic Challenge Today: Primarily from Nonstate Actors?

Potential unified action by Muslim states against Western interests is thus a theoretical possibility but unlikely on any systematic basis. Western states are not likely to permit their relations with the broader Muslim world to deteriorate to such an extent, and Muslim states' own interests are diverse enough to inhibit a common front, except under the gravest of perceived challenges. States themselves may not present the greatest challenge to Western interests, however. The problem may arise more from the actions of radical Islamic movements. After all, the number of states involved in the export of radical Islamic policies are few in the world, limited at the moment to Iran and to a much lesser degree Sudan. Are movements more dangerous than states?

Radical movements operating independently of governments are potentially dangerous on four grounds. First, they can engage in terrorist and criminal acts of violence against Western individuals and targets, both in the Muslim world and on Western soil, more easily than states can conduct these acts. States are answerable, movements are not. Second, they are capable of weakening or damaging moderate governments and leaders in ways that destabilize the Middle East and other regions. Third, they can lend moral, material, and ideological support to other radical movements on the world scene. Fourth, as movements they bear no responsibility for the complex task of conducting governmental affairs; instead they are free to criticize existing governments opportunistically, at will, without regard for political and economic reality.

Western states are both ill-positioned and ill-suited to carry out a direct struggle against radical Islamic organizations by themselves. If radical organizations are engaged in political violence, especially of a transnational nature, Western states will of course treat these issues first and foremost as a police/security issue, maintaining lists of organizations and individuals known to be engaging in clear-cut international violence, denying them access to Western states and institutions, and cooperating with friendly regional states on intelligence relating to the activities. The West can also place international pressure upon those states known to be deliberately harboring and supporting such movements operating internationally. Washington's use of the state-sponsored "terrorist list" is by now a familiar diplomatic instrument. Where Muslim governments share concern with the West over operations by radical Islamist organizations, they too will turn to bilateral cooperation with Western governments to combat them.

The primary responsibility for dealing with radical Islamic organizations lies with the individual Muslim states themselves. Here the issue is not always simple because of the broad gray areas between politics and "terrorism." When the term "terrorism" is invoked, it simplifies the Western problem enormously, for what is labeled terrorism may not need to be dealt with as a complex political problem. In fact, most Islamist organizations are not regularly engaging in international or domestic violence. Often Islamist groups are described by authoritarian regimes as terrorist or radical simply as a pretext to eliminate the political movement as an opposition group. A reality of politics in the contemporary Muslim world is that Islamist organizations are the most likely source of opposition politics to existing regimes; they generally enjoy greater legitimacy in the public eye and have deeper grass-roots bases than other parties. Unless political systems are opened up to a broad variety of competing forces, the Islamists are the most likely inheritors of power when authoritarian regimes break down.

In other cases systematic mishandling of political relationships by the state and the state's use of massive force—often a form of political violence in itself—against Islamist organizations have served to push these organizations into violence. In yet other cases radical groups are fully dedicated to using violence to achieve their goals and are not willing to compromise with established governments. Radical Islamist groups vary considerably, too, in the breadth of their popular base: Some merely represent activities of fringe groups. In most cases, however, they represent broader movements or are linked with a coalition of forces that seek political change, especially where regimes treat Islamist movements primarily as a security problem rather than a political problem. The United States must carefully avoid blanket support to authoritarian regimes that may be mishandling opposition movements and that seek license from Washington to continue violating human rights and curtailing democratic processes in the name of the "struggle against fundamentalism."

Even the use of violence by an organization is not an automatic touchstone for identifying the group as hard-core radical. Certainly the international order appropriately considers the use of violence an unacceptable means of political action in any political system. But where the state itself turns readily to violence and harsh repression, it can often push Islamist groups into violent response whereby both sides can be said to be "employing terror." By definition states are supposed to possess a monopoly over the legitimate right and means to use force and violence, but in unstable political systems, where states enjoy very limited legitimacy, such principles are less clear.

Dealing with the Islamist Challenge

The reality today is that Islamist movements threaten Muslim regimes far more than they threaten Western interests. In an astonishing about-face, Muslim regimes—Egypt, Algeria, Uzbekistan, and Tunisia, among others— are now taking the lead in alerting Washington to the "dangers of fundamentalism." Washington and Arab regimes may thus share a problem about how to cope with Islamist radicalism in the region. But do they share a solution? What, in fact, are the appropriate responses to radical Islamic organizations that challenge the state's authority?

A key source of the problem, as we have noted earlier, are failing regimes that prefer to eliminate opposition movements within the state. Differing aspirations and interests within the body politic irritate the regime and lead to the creation of more pervasive internal security systems and the strengthening of the authoritarian political order. Repressive regimes themselves then generate ideological policies that threaten minorities and neighbors, vitiating yet further any chance for serious unity of purpose. Indeed, both Algeria and Egypt have over the past few years refused serious dialogue with mainstream Islamist organizations.

With the unintended assistance of state mechanisms of repression, Islamist movements have now gained a monopoly over most opposition movements in the Arab world. Where they have been particularly suppressed and persecuted, as in Egypt, Algeria, and Tunisia, they have gained greater mystique, an appeal of the forbidden, a "magical" quality reflecting their ubiquitous and simplistic slogan *"Al-Islam Huwwa al-Hall"* (Islam Is the Solution). Deprived of the opportunity to participate extensively in government, the Islamists have the luxury of proclaiming the "solution" without actually having to demonstrate just what their solution is to so many intractable problems.

The Politics of Inclusion

There is no easy answer about how to cope with the potentially negative, intolerant, anti-Western tendencies of radical Islam, but there are two tasks to be met: The first is to change the more uncompromising policies and attitudes of Islamic movements where possible. Islamist movements are evolving and represent a considerable variety of ideas, tactics, leadership, and goals. It is important for Western and Muslim governments to differentiate among them and deal with them. The second task is to marginalize the more extremist elements in ways that do not increase the use of violence on both sides, a trend that often serves only to strengthen, not weaken, the extremists.

The challenge is not a simple one. In the end, however, both problems can be successfully approached only by a policy of inclusion of Islam into the political system rather than exclusion. Exclusionary policies have simply not worked. Repression has tended to increase the popularity of Islamist movements and to move them in more violent directions as they have been repressed; Egypt and Algeria demonstrate this tendency.

A policy of inclusion is based on the belief that once Islamist movements enter the political process, several different things will happen.

- The movement will have to move beyond facile slogans to declare its position on a variety of difficult issues; it will have to adopt a platform open to public scrutiny.
- What had been strictly a movement will now have to adopt political responsibility via participation; it will not be able to content itself with mere opportunism.
- Islamist politicians will have to deal with others whose principles they do not necessarily accept, forcing them to compromise their abstract principles in the direction of reality.[3]
- Islamist politicians will be forced to take public positions on important issues against which they will be judged at later elections. They will begin to face the problem of answerability and to demonstrate that they have no "magic" answers either.
- Islamist parties will soon fall into "normal perspective" within the political system; that is, they will no longer represent something special but will start to resemble other political parties with their same strengths, weaknesses, mistakes, foibles, and even corruption. This process has in fact happened in Turkey and Pakistan, where Islamist parties are a normal and, very often, unexciting part of the political spectrum.[4]

This strategy, which is designed to change, compromise, and educate the

Islamists, does not deny the possibility that certain skilled Islamist politicians may have something to offer in the political arena. Their presence will considerably broaden the framework of the national debate. Those politicians and policies that contribute something will remain; the impractical and the fatuous will not long survive. In this respect, Jordan is one of the few Arab states that has handled its own Islamist movement wisely in recent years. The Islamists have participated in the democratic process, made an impressive showing at the first elections, but over time demonstrated that they do not have much to offer. Their movement has subsequently weakened (assisted by some deft politics by the king). Although the Islamists will always have supporters, they have lost their magic allure.

Often objections arise that Islamists will support democracy, as nearly all do while in opposition, only to eliminate it when they themselves come to power—the formula known as "one man, one vote, one time." This potential problem has several responses. First, the problem is hardly unique to Islamists. Many political parties in the Arab world and elsewhere have come to power in some kind of elections or by coup claiming they would hold elections but later refusing to hold elections or to leave power peacefully. The problem is not the Islamists but the political culture itself; the unfamiliarity of the democratic process and experience remains a major problem where politics is seen as a zero-sum game. Democracy is a frail commodity in the Muslim world, where many contenders are capable of periodically snuffing it out.

Second, radical parties such as the Islamists must be allowed to enter the process only gradually. If they spring overnight from an underground forbidden status via a strong protest vote into a massive electoral victory, they will gain near total power and will have not been subject to any of the "taming" experiences of sharing in, but not dominating, governance. This was the Algerian experience in the elections in late 1991. Instead, the entry of radical parties must be gradual, perhaps by their gaining control of certain municipalities or a modest proportion in the legislature.[5] Controls over their actions should also be available: a president, an army, a court system, and other mechanisms that will prevent Islamists from gaining total power at the outset and forcing them to work within the existing system.

Finally, states that move to hold free elections must establish an agreed-upon national charter in advance—rules of the game that include the commitment to hold new elections at a scheduled time, protection of minority rights, retention of basic freedoms of speech, recognition of the rule of law, and transparency in internal party decision making. Although there is no guarantee that agreement to such ground rules will be honored later on, adherence to the rules would constitute prima facie evidence of legitimacy, by which the legitimacy of the regime could later be seriously challenged if it failed to honor the agreement. Violation of national charter principles would then engender the opposition of the international community and run the risk of diplomatic and economic sanctions, as has happened in Haiti and Guatemala in 1993. Citizen groups in Egypt, for example, are attempting to create such national charter organizations to encourage a political transition to democracy.

Thus the circumstances and the means by which Islamists attain power are critical determinants of the character of a new Islamist regime: who, where, when, and how. Power achieved by social revolution, as in Iran, represents the worst circumstance under which Islamists can come to power; revolutionary chaos bolsters the power of the most extreme factions in an environment in which other restraints are absent. Islamist victory by coup, as in Sudan, is equally undesirable, for normal restraints on the exercise of power are then also missing, even if the chaos of social revolution is absent. Clearly, power by ballot box offers the best chance to constrain the radicalism of Islamists, or any other radical group, as well as the opportunity to influence their evolution.

The politics of inclusion is not risk-free. Even if Islamist victory comes by way of the ballot box, the international community as well as most Muslims do not want to see another Iran emerge, even if only for five to ten years. Citizens of the state forced to live for a decade or so under a repressive and authoritarian Islamist regime would not deem the risk of elections to have been wise.[6] But risks are deeply inherent in the present political systems as well, with the potential of explosion or social revolution á la Iran if things go very badly under present authoritarian regimes that exclude the Islamists. The sins of past Algerian government policies are now visited upon the present: The armed radical wing of FIS has mushroomed out of the regime's postelection cancellation of the democratic experiment and subsequent repression of the victorious party.

In short, a process of inclusion probably provides greater controls over the Islamist movements than does a policy of exclusion and violent confrontation. But regimes and leaders in power today are not interested in whether inclusion over the longer run will weaken the attraction of radical Islam. They simply do not want to hold elections in which they know they will almost certainly lose power—to anybody, even if the Islamists were not to win. Western policy makers often acknowledge that the politics of inclusion might be successful over the longer run, but these same governments are usually interested only in managing the short term; no one wants the experiment on his watch. By this reasoning, it often appears more attractive and safer to permit local repression of Islamist forces over the short run in the hope that the movement will eventually weaken or go away. Few cases support this hope.[7]

A case can be made that victory by the Islamists, even by the ballot box, as might happen in Algeria or Egypt, still leaves a large Westernized minority, including most of the elites, totally alienated under strict Islamic law, even if this law is imposed in a relatively nonauthoritarian manner. The Westernized class itself might rebel or plot the overthrow of the regime simply to rid itself of unwelcome and alien philosophies of government and social practice they would view as retrogressive. This dilemma is real, but it is inherent in almost any process of change in the Muslim world, where entrenched elites are reluctant to give up power to the masses in open elections and fear the results of power exercised in the name of another social class. Indeed, the dilemma is unavoidable and will almost certainly be part of any process of political liberalization in the region, whether or not the Islamists win. The choice may be between the dislocations of an Islamic government and the dislocations of repression that may eventually lead to greater instability. It is important to remember that the Islamists themselves partly, but not exclusively, represent a vehicle for class protest and change. In short, other elements are involved in this phenomenon besides religious politics.

Islamism as a Nonideological Movement

Much analysis of Islamist movements focuses on their ideology and world vision, yet a study must emphasize nonideological components of the Islamist movement as well. Political movements attract a variety of different followers operating from different motivations. For some the expressed ideology and philosophy of the party is the magnet; for others it may reflect an opportunistic drive for the power and position the party affords. For yet others it may be a vehicle of regional, ethnic, tribal, religious, or class power in which the actual ideology is simply the traditional ideology of that group, inherited and accepted without much thought. These regional, tribal, or clan affiliations, for example, considerably affect the political allegiances of members within the various Egyptian or Algerian Islamist groups.

These factors are highly localized and difficult for the outsider to fully fathom. They are important to consider, however, since the political dynamic of these organizations will then reflect more than just ideological issues or the welfare of the country at large: The bonds of association and their party's interests will always remain a separate factor in the group's thinking, regardless of the circumstances of the country. Mere improvement in the economic and social conditions alone, therefore, will not nullify the interests of clan or class groups and their desire for greater power within the system. Islamist parties in part represent such class interests, among other things. Even if they do so, class or clan groups will not necessarily find the Islamists the most congenial or effective vehicle for their political and economic ambitions.

Islam as a Catalyst for Have-Not States

A key challenge to the international system in the next decades will be the large numbers of Third World and ex-communist states struggling to come to terms with long-overdue reform in the political and economic sphere and with their place in the international economy. They perceive themselves under assault from three reigning ideas of the Western political system: free market capitalism, secular democracy and human rights, and the nation-state as the basic unit of international relations. The West, particularly in the aftermath of the Cold War, powerfully advocates these concepts, both explicitly and implicitly. Yet for all their long-term validity as a basis for a new world order, these ideas will likely prove ineffective in meeting the needs of most Third World and postcommunist states for some time to come. In simple terms, they will not deliver in the short to medium term for states under heavy pressure from their populations for quick, tangible improvement of economic and social life.

Indeed, considerable danger derives from the likelihood that many Third World states—only some of them Muslim—will be increasingly marginalized and excluded from broader patterns of international trade. Simply put, some states may simply become irrelevant to the world economy: They lack the funds to buy, and they have nothing significant to sell. Harshly put, if they were to disappear the world economy would not notice.[8] States may simply be unable to succeed because of political and economic mismanagement for which they themselves are largely responsible, or because of larger market forces, or as a result of general underdevelopment and shortage of resources. Pressures upon undeveloped states will grow as the world economy becomes more integrated and dependent on information flow and technical and scientific expertise. As one prominent Egyptian thinker puts it,

The contemporary world is divided into two camps: one comprising those who have succeeded in crossing the critical threshold and who are confident that they can master not only their own fate but that of the entire planet; the other comprising those who remain below the critical threshold and who have lost any hope of regaining control over their destiny. . . . Those beneath the threshold are likely to constitute an ever-growing percentage of the global population while becoming more and more marginalized, alienated and downtrodden.[9]

This kind of economic future—many in the Third World will view it as Darwinian—may create a growing category of states that will qualify in one sense or another simply as losers on the international scene. Their existence creates a pool of disadvantaged states who are potentially susceptible to consolidation against the West in an intensified form of North-South struggle. As one stark commentator says:

When the notion of Progress was invented in the eighteenth century the wealth gap between "North" and "South" was about 2 to 1. After the Second World War it was about 40 to 1. Today it is nearly 70 to 1. . . . An increasingly globalized, integrated economy generates world-wide social structures reminiscent of apartheid. . . .

The brave new planetary economy can probably provide relative security for all but about 15–20 percent of the citizens of the industrialized countries, but will be unable to integrate more than a third, roughly speaking, of the people in the euphemistically entitled "developing" countries.

Under the circumstances it is hardly surprising that people are massively seeking shelter in primitive or violent demands for identity based on a variety of fundamentalist programs. How else can they be expected to defend themselves in the absence of a strong, unifying and relatively beneficent state, when they are not members of the transnational elite?[10]

The crises of numerous Muslim states involves many of these elements— crises in economics, politics, and national unity—even if they do not fall into the category of near hopeless cases described above. We have already discussed the failure of regimes to undertake political reform and the external pressures of democratization and observance of human rights upon them. Yet it is important to note the strong degree of ambivalence among Muslim publics.

Pressure for democratization will be opposed by nearly all present governments that lack clear democratic legitimacy; they will feel threatened and weakened by policies that force them into power sharing, limitation of their authority over the security apparatus, reforms that strengthen the opposition, or elections they cannot win. Dominant social groups, even those hostile to present rulers, may fear political change that too sharply alters the status quo from which they benefit.

On the other hand, pressure for democratization will be welcomed by those who seek change in present regimes and rulers; by those who seek protection of their human rights from abusive governments, including Islamists; by those who feel excluded from the present system; and by those who wish excluded ethnic, sectarian, regional, or class groups to gain new power in society. The challenge of Western norms with regard to democracy and human rights is thus highly complex and presents a double-edged sword. This issue is one of the most sensitive and important for the Middle East and elsewhere over the long term.

The Western concept of the nation-state brings yet another severe problem to most states: For the majority are not nation-states at all but states with mixed ethnic or religious populations; consequently, they are threatened by active or potential separatist movements and face constant dissatisfaction from violation of minority and human rights. The post–Cold War international environment is far less tolerant of these conditions, and the West is taking the lead in imposing penalties on states that violate established principles of human rights.

Under these domestic strains, coupled with the new strains imposed by the international environment, a backlash to the Western-dominated order is developing. Its extent and depth is not yet clear. Islamist movements are one of the most prominent forms of expression of this backlash, although Islamism also embraces concepts such as the issue of the role of Western states in the history of the Muslim world. Partly for this reason it has become popular to suggest that Islam is indeed the next "ism" the West will confront now that communism has fallen.

Under these circumstances afflicted Third World states as a whole may seek greater coordination of policies among themselves to resist what they perceive as a world order largely set against their interests. As these beleaguered states seek leadership for their cause, a "role in search of an actor" inevitably emerges, as Gamal Abdel Nasser once put it. What state might take up this role? Historically, a variety of left-wing movements have supported the cause of "oppressed" states. The Soviet Union manipulated and sometimes supported these forces. The nonaligned movement was also closely linked with them.

Islamist ideology may represent the most advanced international movement in formulating a broad and coherent set of grievances against the West
and the "Western-dominated" international system. They are followed by the
far less systematically developed arguments of several East Asian nations,
most notably Singapore's Lee Kuan Yew and his foreign minister, Bilahari
Kausikan. The latter harshly speculates that the Western approach to human
rights is

> ideological, not empirical. The West needs its myths to live by; missionary
> zeal to whip the heathen along the path of righteousness and remake the
> world in its own image is deeply ingrained in Western (especially
> American) political culture. . . . [This comes from] if not exactly a
> "declining" West, then at least a West flushed with victory over its Cold
> War adversary but unable to compete economically, unwilling to come to
> grips with many of its own serious economic and social problems, all too
> prone to blame others for its own failings, and exhausted of everything
> except pretensions of special virtue.[11]

He is joined in these sentiments by Prime Minister Mahathir of Malaysia, as
well as by Chinese rejection of Western values as nonuniversal.

It is striking that the growing opposition to Western political ideals is now
emerging from two of the oldest and most coherent alternative civilizations.
It is also striking that Singapore, Malaysia, and China are actually faring well
in the international economic order, even if threatened to some extent in the
political and cultural sphere, and yet are adopting common positions with
many aspects of Islamic thinking. They are *theoretically* in a position to make
common cause with other states, especially Muslim states, to oppose strong
Western pressures and ideological concepts.

If there is any trend toward coalescence of states dissatisfied with the basic
foundations of post–Cold War international relations, which states might seek
leadership? Iran, the first modern Islamist state, is the only one to have created a well-developed Islamic framework of ideas relating to the "liberation of
the oppressed." Iran's Shi'ite political vocabulary already regularly employs
the concept of the oppressed *(Mustadh'afin)*, vulnerable before the "arrogant of
the world" *(Mustakbarin)*, as part of a broader Islamic liberation theology.
Indeed, in the late 1970s, before the Iranian revolution and in the early years
after it, several ideological strains competed among Iran's Islamists. The
Iranian Mojahedin-e-Khalq movement, Khomeini's most serious competitor

for power (later to be brutally crushed by Khomeini in favor of rule by the clergy), espoused a form of Islamic Marxism in which God was seen as the creator of the just universe, in which Islam bears a historic revolutionary mission to overthrow oppression and establish a just state free of exploitation.[12]

In the early years after the revolution Tehran originally extended the concept of the oppressed to all the "oppressed states of the world," namely, Third World states, but it had difficulty in exporting its ideas beyond the Muslim world and, indeed, sometimes encountered problems in moving beyond the world of Shi'ites into the Sunni Muslim world itself. As late as September 1993, in response to the Palestinian-Israeli initial memorandum of understanding, Iran suggested:

> The West is out to impose a new Middle East order, and the PLO-Israeli accord is the first step. Iran must not sit idly by. One way to counter American influence would be to form an alliance with Asian countries like China and India. . . . It can counter the pressure . . . also by forming an alliance of Islamic, leftist and nationalist movements.[13]

Iran is severely hindered, however, by its Shi'ite and Persian character, which often alienates majority Sunni and Arab activists, at least in granting Iran a leadership role. The Iranian state is regarded by all Islamists with great interest, though especially for its extraordinary accomplishment in overthrowing the West's chief ally in the Middle East and in backing the most successful of Muslim guerrilla movements, the Shi'ite groups of Lebanon which contributed to the withdrawal of Western and Israeli forces from the country in the mid-1980s.

How likely is it that other Islamist states will seek this role for themselves? As the first Sunni Islamist state, Sudan under its present Islamist-military leadership has had only modest intellectual impact so far and lacks international prominence and wealth, despite its willingness to provide havens for banned Islamist leaders in the region. Its leading figure of the Islamist movement, Hasan al-Turabi, is one of the outstanding spokesmen for Islamism in the contemporary world. Turabi has organized a series of conferences in Khartoum, inviting Islamist parties and other anti–status quo secular radicals as well. Turabi is exceedingly ambitious for his program and sees himself as the preeminent spokesman for Sunni Islamist movements in the Muslim world. His party came to power in Khartoum in 1989 through a military coup by officers associated with his movement.

The Sudanese case is important precisely because it is the first Islamist victory by military coup. The coup was hardly some fortuitous event for the Islamists. Turabi had been building his movement and base of support for decades in strategic elements of the population. He helped build and utilize an extensive network of Islamic banks with the active support of Saudi Arabia; this network enabled him to build an economic base of support and to direct monies toward establishing support for his movement among a new class of merchants and businessmen. He built ties within the military when his movement was asked by then-President Numayri to instruct the officer corps in Islamic theology. He gained influence over national educational institutions to lend support to his own ideological followers so that loyal students spotted during high school years would be accepted either into university or the military academy.[14] Thus what was a minority movement that could never have taken power by way of the ballot box was in a strong position to come to power through influence over the key power centers of the nation. This approach has attracted the attention of other Islamist movements in North Africa.

Not surprisingly, Iran and Sudan have established close relations as fellow Islamist states, creating considerable anxiety among neighboring countries and in the West as to what "multiplier" effect this combination of states might produce. Despite a strengthening of ideological ties and increased contacts among regional Islamist movements partly facilitated by Sudan, it seems unlikely that either has a truly significant impact on the strength of Islamist movements in Egypt, Algeria, Tunisia, Jordan, the West Bank, Gaza, or which have powerful domestic roots independent of outside support.

The demonstration effect cannot be discounted, however, and were Algeria or Egypt to be taken over by Islamist parties, the political impact on the region—a kind of domino effect—could be considerable as publics perceived that perhaps the old order was crumbling everywhere.

Even the more coherent Islamist ideologies and their criticisms of the Western order are hemmed in by Islam itself: Basically Islamist movements can have impact only among Muslims. Indeed, such movements are perceived with antipathy by most non-Muslim elements who might share a critique of the West but do not wish to see Islam, or perhaps any other religion, as a supreme political force. Nonetheless, it is possible to imagine other prominent states unhappy with the status quo joining forces in an informal alliance to gain leverage in influencing the evolution of the new world order and in attempting to weaken a perceived Western monopoly over it.

Other potential have-not leaders could emerge in China, India, or even Russia under a change of government, but so far none has moved seriously in this direction; indeed, all are so far more intent on competing on the terms of the developed world. As failure stalks the reform efforts of postcommunist states, at least over the short to medium term, and in many other Third World states, we must anticipate that some state or group of states might well seek to pick up this gauntlet of leadership of the countries languishing on the rack in the new world order. Radical Muslim states could well be a prime source, a center of effort, of this broader movement, at least within the Muslim world, especially if one or more major Arab states join the ranks. The cause is there; it is simply waiting for some kind of leadership.

Potential Islamist Policies Toward the West

A key question for the West is: What kind of policies might Islamist governments adopt, especially toward the West, once they achieve power? As we noted earlier, the character of Islamist governments in power depends heavily on how they come to power: by ballot, by bullet, or by barricades? Is their power absolute, or is it constitutionally and institutionally constrained? Which Islamists? Who are the specific leaders, and what are their personalities? Are they radical ideologues or pragmatic politicians? Is the new government secure or under constant internal and external assault? How desperate were the economic, political, and social conditions before the Islamists came to power? What country are we speaking of, and what is its historical, cultural, and geopolitical legacy?

The answers to these questions will profoundly affect the character of the Islamist regime, for even in ideological terms considerable debate exists on such issues as the means of coming to power; the desirability of democracy both before coming to power and after coming to power; the degree of checks and balances within government; the degree of freedom of speech (what about Salman Rushdie?); the right of the people and their representatives to pass laws that contradict ostensible Islamic prohibitions (such as the ban on consumption of alcoholic beverages); the rights of non-Muslim minorities within the state; whether Shari'a law should be completely adopted, partially adopted, or augmented by other Western bodies of law; how deeply Islamic banking will be applied and how it will affect the economy; the legitimate bases of taxation; the position of women in society; the degree of rule of law; and so on.

Most of these issues do not directly affect relations with the West, although the answer to such questions will profoundly affect the psychology and spirit of the Islamic regime in dealing with foreign, and especially Western, states. Foreign policy questions will inevitably involve at least the following issues:

1. *Policy toward Israel.* Will the Islamists continue the state's policy toward Israel before their coming to power or will they reverse it? Will the state declare war against Israel, refuse to recognize it and ignore it, offer minimal recognition (cold peace), or come to terms with it as reality? These questions are already relevant for the Palestinian Islamist Hamas Party, which in April 1994 began to recognize the reality of the coming Palestinian-Israeli settlement and chose not to position itself outside of the debate in coming elections. Iran, too, although strongly opposed to the peace process, is prepared to deal with the reality that its close ally Syria may settle with Jerusalem. Few Islamist states could afford to go to war with Israel under any circumstances and would likely be isolated in such a policy. Practical Islamists offer indicators that the issue of Israel's presence will always remain ideologically significant, but that any practical approach to the problem will have to be postponed indefinitely. Full diplomatic relations between Israel and an Islamist state seem highly unlikely.

2. *Oil Policy.* It is unlikely that any Islamist regime will radically change current practices with regard to production and pricing. All oil-producing states are under heavy pressures to maximize revenue, and resulting world overproduction is not likely to permit a dramatic rise in price.[15] The state's basic interest in oil policy will not change significantly under Islamist leadership (there has been no major change in Iranian oil policy, for example). If any Muslim oil state would ever be likely to invoke the oil weapon against Western producers, however, an Islamist state would be the most likely candidate, especially in the context of regional crises.

3. *International Cooperation on UN Security Council Issues.* In principle, an Islamist state would be inclined to oppose active interventionist policies by Western states under UN auspices. On the other hand, attitudes would depend considerably on the issue. Iran tacitly supported UN-U.S. action against its neighbor Iraq in the 1990–91 Gulf War (Sudan did not) and tacitly supports UN sanctions against Iraq. United Nations action in support of Bosnia's Muslims would almost certainly find support among both radical and moderate Muslim regimes. Ultimately, national interests will often override ideological considerations.

4. *Proliferation of Weapons of Mass Destruction.* Islamist states will be strongly

nationalist almost by definition and will therefore be inclined to policies that strengthen the state, including acquisition of sophisticated conventional weapons and weapons of mass destruction. Yet confronted by
the reality of proliferation in neighboring states and in the region, they
may well revert to a pragmatic self-interest that conceivably could
include support for international agreements limiting the spread of
destructive weaponry.

5. *Regional Security Issues.* Islamist states are likely to oppose the involvement of Western or external states in regional security arrangements,
   which they would interpret as neo-imperialist in character. However,
   Iran has felt ambivalent about U.S. involvement in drawing the line
   against Saddam Hussein in the Gulf. Pragmatic recognition of national
   interests may again temper ideological predispositions.

6. *Free Markets and International Trade.* Nothing in Islam in principle predis-
   poses it to state control of the economy or hostility to private commerce,
   private ownership of property, and the means of production. Most
   Islamist movements today share Western views on these issues.

   Some more radical versions of Islamist thinking do exist, however.
   The Iranian Mojahedin-e-Khalq, for example, have introduced serious
   strains of Marxist thinking into a revisionist Islamist vision that would
   almost surely be strongly statist in many respects.[16] Yet the two Islamist
   states in operation today, Iran and Sudan, both respect private property
   and have a dominant, vibrant private sector.

   There is no reason to believe this essentially capitalist outlook upon
   the economy would differ markedly under most future Islamist
   regimes. Several caveats are nonetheless in order. Political impulses
   could easily lead to seizure of foreign property in situations of political
   confrontation. Such acts would spring from the political culture and not
   from Islam, might emerge from sharp confrontation between Western
   states and the Islamist regime on other grounds. In short, there is no
   reason to believe that Islamist regimes should not be acceptable partners for trade or even investment, in principle. But Islamist regimes will
   be more sensitive to perceived Western dominance of the international
   economic order and more prone to resisting some of its pressures. Such
   regimes are also likely to gravitate toward Third World solidarity on
   economic issues, probably limited mostly to rhetoric. They are likely to
   be realistic about the global economic order and recognize that there
   are few alternatives, but like strongly nationalist regimes, they will be
   prickly, sensitive to slights and to issues of sovereignty.

7. *Human Rights.* Islamist states will face serious problems in bringing Islamic legislation into line with international practice on human and minority rights. Although these issues are primarily domestic in nature, they are now also subjects of international concern and monitoring and no longer within the pure purview of national sovereignty. This area of concern presents a key clash with Islamic law in which the focus is primarily upon the individual's duties to the community and to the state in a just society. Islamic law, while providing legal procedures to ensure fairness in the application of the law, does not have a developed corpus of thinking and procedure relating to the rights of the individual in opposition to the state. Such a corpus could be developed on the basis of existing law, but the debate among Islamists relates, among other things, to conservative jurists' insistence on the precedence of Shari'a law over man-made constitutional law.

Not all Muslim jurists agree there has to be a contradiction between the two in principle. But neither Iran nor Sudan, the two Islamist states on the scene today, have adequately coped with this problem.[17] (Nor have most secular governments in the Third World either—again suggesting we are partly dealing with political culture as much as with religious law.) In terms of minority rights, Islamic human rights schemes elaborated so far this century "do not provide real protection for the rights of religious minorities comparable to those found in international human rights law."[18] As a result, future Islamist governments are likely to run into confrontations with international practice and receive considerable international pressure. The more these regimes are perceived to be hostile to the West in other respects, the more they will be singled out for pressure—as Sudan— in relation to other violators in countries more friendly to the West.

8. *Domestic Redistribution Policies.* Any radical movement requires adoption of some element of redistributive philosophy, at least initially, partly as a means of consolidating power by lending economic benefits and power to their supporters. Islamists have not been particularly inclined toward redistributive policies in their economic doctrines in either Iran or Sudan. Nor is there anything in Islam that is supportive of broad redistributive policies apart from a general sense of social compassion.

Nonetheless, some future Islamic movement could well move in the direction of more redistributive policies once in power. Many of these states face powerful economic and social challenges not easily handled, with populations expecting alleviation of their worst problems. It will be difficult for any Islamist group coming to power not to adopt populist policies to meet needs and demands, which suggest elements of redistribution—at least initially—as one answer. Also, there is no philosophic bar to Islamist states calling for redistributive policies on an international level to challenge what they perceive as unjust economic consequences of the "Western-imposed" world order. Indeed, this kind of language is already present in many commentaries on the West. Such rhetoric will have limited impact unless combined with similar grievances from a variety of other states. Differing economic interests will likely prevent most Muslim states from allying on the issue of international redistribution policies.

In sum, not all Islamist regimes are destined to be truly radical in their policies once in power, even if their predisposition is toward more negative (and often ignorant) views of the West. As Islamist movements or parties participate in the political process, they recognize that they must develop more realistic and nuanced views toward a whole range of issues, including how they wish to conduct unavoidable political and economic relations with the West. A learning and maturation process is underway. Over time, most Islamist parties or regimes are likely to develop more pragmatic approaches to international realities. Nonetheless, the tenor of Western relations with them could remain prickly for some period of time, in the same way as relations are often touchy with hypersensitive new nationalist movements.

Notes

1. *Mideast Mirror,* June 28, 1993, p. 18.

2. See Said, *Orientalism,* for example.

3. The prospect of upcoming elections on the West Bank, for example, may force the radical Hamas movement to abandon its rigid rejectionist posture on peace with Israel and to move toward greater realism in accepting the reality of the upcoming settlement. Hamas has not accepted Israel, but it wants to be part of postsettlement politics, in which relations with Israel are the political reality. See Amman's daily *Al-Ra'i* and *Jordan Times* analysis as quoted in *Mideast Mirror,* April 21, 1994, p. 12.

4. In the Turkish municipal elections of March 1994, Turkey's main Islamist

party, the Refah (Welfare) Party, won the mayoralty by a small plurality in Istanbul and Ankara. Traditional Ataturkist secularists have expressed considerable dismay at this outcome, in which Refah had better grass-roots organization and benefited from public disillusionment with other parties. The challenge to Refah will now be considerable. It must deal effectively with huge economic and social problems in both cities, it cannot challenge the democratic structure of the state without certain army intervention, and it cannot risk alienating those who cast their ballots for other parties through radical new restrictive policies without potential severe backlash. In short, the challenge is as much to Refah and its future credibility as it is to the state and a sceptical public.

5. Algeria has already experienced some Islamist control of municipalities, where the experience was not a disaster, but where continuing political deterioration led only to further strengthening on the national level. Some Algerians claim that the Islamists used the experience to strengthen their own cadres by use of local funds distributed to supporters. (Such a practice sounds familiar, known in the West—but inappropriately for Islam—as "pork-barrel politics.") Turkey, as noted in the footnote above, faces the same experience. The experience might also be compared to communists coming to power during the Cold War in Italian cities, or in Calcutta, West Bengal Province, and Kerala in India. The local communist parties made numerous mistakes in rule (hardly new in local politics), but the situation never became disastrous; a total communist takeover of either country, on the other hand, would have elicited immense international alarm.

6. After the Algerian military in January 1992 annulled the elections won by the Islamists (FIS) rather than allow them to accede to power, King Hassan in neighboring Morocco remarked that it would have been interesting to see what the Islamists would actually have done in power. Many Algerians reply to all who offer such comments, "Thanks, but we don't want to be your social laboratory."

7. Tunisian leaders believe they have acted wisely in repressing their country's leading Islamist party, al-Nahda, whose seemingly moderate leader, Rashid al-Ghannushi, has fled to London. The Tunisian authorities argue that such a step was necessary while Tunisia was passing through a transitional period of economic hardship; that indicators suggest that the economy will begun an upturn shortly, after which time the Islamists will lose their appeal and political liberalization can then resume. Possibly, but the jury is still out.

Most regimes that promise liberalization "after things get better" are usually deceiving themselves, and others. If Tunisian postponement of liberalization until things are better is a successful policy, it would probably still not apply to Algeria and Egypt with their far deeper and more intractable problems.

8. See discussion of this topic by Robert Heilbronner, "Growth and the Lumpen Planet," *New Perspectives Quarterly,* Spring 1993, p. 48–53.

9. Mohamed Sid-Ahmed, "Cybernetic Colonialism and the Moral Search," *New Perspectives Quarterly,* Spring 1994, pp. 16–17.

10. Susan George, "One-Third In, Two-Thirds Out." *New Perspectives Quarterly,* Spring 1993, pp. 53–54.

11. Bilahari Kausikan, "East and Southeast Asia and the Post–Cold War International Politics of Human Rights," *Studies in Conflict and Terrorism,* Vol. 16, 1993, p. 250.

12. Ervand Abrahamian, *The Iranian Mojahedin* (New Haven, CT: Yale University Press, 1989), pp. 92–98.

13. *Mideast Mirror,* September 21, 1993, p. 22.

14. For excellent discussions of this process, see Abbashar Jamal, "Funding Fundamentalism: The Political Economy of an Islamist State," and Ali Abdalla Abbas,"The National Islamic Front and the Politics of Education," in *Middle East Report,* September 1991. Also see Carol Fluehr-Lobban, "Islamization in Sudan: A Critical Assessment," in John O. Voll, ed., *Sudan: State and Society in Crisis* (Indiana University Press, 1991).

15. Based on the views of Eliyahu Kanovsky, the Israeli oil analyst whose analyses over the years have been demonstrably prescient.

16. See Abrahamian, *The Iranian Mojahedin,* pp. 145–149.

17. For an outstanding discussion of this problem see Ann Elizabeth Mayer, *Islam and Human Rights: Tradition and Politics* (Boulder, CO: Westview Press, 1991), especially pp. 43–72.

18. Ibid, p. 160.

8

THE GEOPOLITICAL DIMENSION

Areas of Confrontation

The cultural borders of Islam—its "cultural faultlines"—span a broad part of the world. The arc of the Muslim world reaches from the Straits of Gibraltar east along the length of the Mediterranean, up through the Balkans, the Black Sea, across the Caucausus and southern Russia, down through Western China, across India (as a minority population), along the Burmese border with Bangladesh, through southern Thailand, Malaysia, and down into Indonesia and parts of the Philippines. Islam also has its southern borders in Africa, where Islamic Africa extends down into the Sahel, West Africa, as well as deep south along the East African coast. Most of the civilizations that border Islam are Christian, but not all—especially in East Asia, where Islam borders Hinduism, Buddhism, and Confucianism, and in Africa, where it adjoins animist faiths viewed by Islamists as prime recruitment areas.

Those who express visceral cultural anxieties about Islam, such as Samuel Huntington, speak of Islam's "bloody borders."[1] Indeed, strategic and cultural conflict has taken place on these borders over many centuries. They are hardly unique as places of confrontation, however; world history is replete with bloody borders across East Asia, Western Europe, the pre-Islamic Near East, Latin America, and Africa. If it comes to ethnic stereotyping, white Europeans are the most culpable in terms of blood spilled in conflict, certainly in the twentieth century. Apart from the emotive value of talking of "bloody borders," such a description tells us very little about the nature of such conflicts in the coming century. Conflict can emerge at virtually any sort of cultural border.

But the flashpoints along the Islamic march-lands do require analysis. How similar are they in nature from region to region? Are Islamic sentiments the common characteristic in sparking conflict? In fact, there are many differing factors that combine in different ways, in different areas, to produce friction. And conflict is not limited to the borders where Islam meets other civilizations but extends to areas within the Islamic world itself and, of course, within non-Islamic regions.

What broad types of interaction exist between Islam and non-Islam around the world? They can be roughly categorized as

- separatism—the breaking away of Muslim regions from non-Muslim regions;
- irridentism—the desire to extend state control over Muslim areas under the control of an ethnically or religiously different state;
- Muslim anger at former imperial control exercised over it: Roman Catholic, Orthodox Christian, Buddhist, Confucian, Hindu;
- anger and resentment by other religious and ethnic groups at former Muslim imperial control over them;
- border disputes between Muslim and non-Muslim states;
- the struggle for assertion of power by Muslim minorities within non-Muslim majoritarian states;
- real or perceived economic dominance and political discrimination by non-Muslims over Muslims;
- proselytization and propagation of the Islamic faith in non-Muslim areas;
- fear by non-Muslims with weak social structures of the power of Islamic social institutions.

Let us look at each region briefly to identify these dynamic factors of conflict and the degree of Islam's role among them.

The Mediterranean

Over most of the past century the Mediterranean has been the border between colonizer and colonized, the administrators and the subjects of European imperialism. Colonialism is the primary historical fact about the nature of this geographical confrontation. What distinguishes trans-Mediterranean colonialism on the one hand from French colonialism in Africa or British colonialism in South Asia on the other is that the Mediterranean represents an immediate, "contiguous" sea border with Europe. There is no escaping the geographical intimacy of these unequal colonial relationships and its memories—more powerful than any specific cultural clash. The Middle Eastern people, especially along the

Mediterranean, have simply experienced Europe longer than have other people of the world. The modern period has indeed added new issues to the friction across the waters such as migration, weapons proliferation, trade restrictions, and political violence. Otherwise there is today almost no territorial conflict, irredentism, or subversion between Europe and North Africa, or any "border skirmishes." War is not a high likelihood. Islam's contact across the Mediterranean is, furthermore, primarily with Roman Catholicism, except for the eastern Mediterranean. Islam's borders with Roman Catholicism are essentially stable, whereas those with other religions are not.

The West's concerns in North Africa have little to do with Islam per se so much as the syndrome of North-South problems that can negatively affect Western Europe.

Turkey's Borders with "Christian" States in the Balkans

Turkey is the focal point of Islam in contact with southeastern Europe. But relations in this region are complicated by the existence of another, important cultural divide: between Eastern and Western Christianity. As noted earlier, Eastern Christianity historically developed in intimate connection with ethnicity, producing a proliferation of ethnocultural Orthodox churches, each using distinct liturgical languages. Thus the Orthodox Church in its many varieties came to be a primary vehicle of nationalism in the region, initially often more hostile toward Rome and the Pope than toward Islam itself. After the conflict with Rome began to recede in the face of the Ottoman challenge and occupation of the Balkans in the fourteenth century, Orthodox churches were required to work closely with Ottoman administrators. It was ultimately the Orthodox churches that helped define and preserve national entities and fuel the struggle for the independence of the various Christian states in the Balkans in the nineteenth and twentieth centuries. The Orthodox churches thus have a significant history of close—and confrontational—dealings with Islam within their societies. This experience differs sharply with the western Mediterranean fault line, which is Roman Catholic and where the imperialists were the Christians. In the Balkans the imperialists were the Muslims.

It is the regions where the Orthodox churches hold influence today that have the keenest sense of the existence of "Christendom" as a living phenomenon, still counterpoised against Islam. The Eastern Christian–Islamic borderland represents probably the most intense and emotional point of Christian "cultural clash" with Islam on the world scene. Here, too, is a kind of "colonial legacy," but in reverse, for not only have these cultures clashed with each other but Christian populations were subordinate to the Muslim Ottoman Empire for many centuries. Relationships of inequality, ruler and ruled, have thus characterized the region, first Muslim over Christian, and now reversed to a degree today with the sometimes higher educational and technical levels of some Balkan states over Muslim ones.

Thus relations between Turkey and Bulgaria, Turkey and Greece, Turkey and Orthodox Serbia and even Romania, all carry much historical baggage from the past. This fact helps account for much of the reawakened passion of the Bosnian conflict. The breakup of the Soviet Empire in Eastern Europe has intensified the conflict in the Balkans, where not only is there much unfinished business among Christians of the region (Orthodox Serb versus Catholic Croat) but the Islamic element is drawn in: the Muslims of Bosnia and the situation of the Muslims of Kosovo, poised to explode, where Serbia is pitted against Albania. Irredentist issues are also present between Turkey and Greece, Turkey and Bulgaria, and Turkey and Armenia, including some territorial claims against Turkey by Christians. Conflict flares not only between Christian and Muslims but between Catholic and Orthodox as well, indicating that Islam is not the determinative factor in Balkan conflicts.

Despite the religious passions unleashed in the Balkans, it is striking to note that U.S. opinion, and some European opinion, is basically unmoved by the religious facet of Balkan problems. Contrary to the (uninformed) expectations of most Muslims, the West has in fact demonstrated far greater sympathy for the victimized Muslims of Bosnia than for either the Catholic Croats or the Orthodox Christian Serbs, who are dominant. Clearly the modern secular West judges the issue primarily on the more objective basis of its legal and humanitarian aspects rather than on religious affinity. The absence of a strong sense of sectarian kinship on the part Americans and many West Europeans in the conflict is thus a highly important observation in the context of "the West versus Islam."[2] It is, furthermore, noteworthy that Jews in the West, while mindful of Islam's conflict with Israel, are among the most vocal supporters of Western action to prevent genocide against the Bosnian Muslims.

In addition to historical-psychological factors, the major concerns in this Balkan–southeastern European–Caucasus region today are territorial, unlike the North African border with Europe, with considerable prospect for expansion of the ongoing war(s). Refugee problems produced by the conflict are also a factor of stress. In the Crimea the Muslim Crimean Tatars, exiled as a whole people by Stalin during World War II, today seek restoration of their

lands now in the hands of Russians and Ukrainians; but in the Crimea con-
flict between Christians themselves—Russians and Ukrainians in the
Crimea—is far more intense than between the Muslim Tatars and the
Christians. In the Caucasus Orthodox Armenians are at war with Muslim
Azerbaijanis, but mostly over the modern irredentist issue of Nagorniy
Karabakh, an Armenian enclave inside the borders of Azerbaijan, whose ill-
conceived borders Stalin drew arbitrarily. The Armenian-Azerbaijani conflict
is therefore primarily more territorial than religious, just as are other territorial conflicts in the Caucasus, particularly those in Georgia that are primarily
among Christians (the Abkhaz and Ossetians), rather than between Muslims
and Christians.

Central Asia

The bloodiest conflict in Central Asia today is the civil war in Tajikistan—
ideological, ethnic, and regional in character—taking place almost exclusively
among Muslims, that is, between Uzbeks and Tajiks, and among Tajiks themselves. Russia proper has only one major external border with Islam, its borders with Muslim Kazakhstan. The latent prospects for conflict between the
Orthodox Russians and Muslim Kazakhs are high, although the reasons are
almost purely nationalist, over territory and power, not religion. The Kazakhs
in fact have a weakly developed sense of Islam and are primarily motivated
by a desire to regain Kazakh ethnic control over their own state mechanism
and territory, in which they are at present only the largest minority (41 percent) because of past Russian policies of settling Kazakh lands with ethnic
Russians. Islam is almost never invoked in the conflict.

Here too, then, we have familiar and classic patterns of colonial relationships deeply resented by the former victims. Yet not only Muslims were victimized by Russian imperialism. These same concerns are shared by other
suppressed nationalities in the former Soviet Union: Ukrainians,
Belorussians, the Baltic peoples, Georgians, and Armenians, all of whom are
Christian. Issues of Russian economic dominance and historic Kazakh
inequality vis-à-vis Russians also affect the Kazakh conflict, although the
Kazakhs for the first time are now in a position to discriminate against the
rights and position of Russians inside Kazakhstan. Over time there will probably be serious conflict over power in Kazakhstan between the Kazakhs and
the large ethnic Russian population (39 percent). This confrontation, still
modest at present, could take on genuine ethnoreligious character if relations

deteriorate sufficiently. Here, too, it is interesting to note that the Islamic element in Russian-Kazakh cultural differences are stressed almost not at all. But Islam (and Russian Orthodoxy) *could* enter the picture if the clash intensifies to the point where each ethnic group reaches deep into its culture to draw forth symbols of legitimacy and cultural authenticity to press its claims—classic cases of religion being consciously used to buttress political ends, even when religion had very little to do with the initial struggle. Thus, if and when serious conflict comes to Russia's borders with Islam, it will be for reasons that hardly originate from Islam but could eventually be exacerbated by Islam if it is brought in as a heavy cannon in the conflict.

In addition to the concrete economic and territorial aspects of Russian-Muslim conflict in Central Asia is a cultural-psychological legacy as well. From the thirteenth to the fifteenth centuries, Russians themselves were dominated by the Mongol-Tatars, who evolved into a Turco-Mongol-Tatar-Islamic civilization just south of the Russian homeland. Russia has been struggling and expanding against these Turco-Tatar forces for centuries. Russian folk memories thus run deep of a nebulous "Asiatic Yellow Peril" that embraces not only China but the power of Islamic peoples to the south.

Russia today clearly worries about Islamic fundamentalism. Not only can it potentially turn the former Muslim republics against Russia; it can also encourage separatist attitudes among the Muslim populations within the Russian federation itself, primarily in Tatarstan and Bashkortistan as well as in the northern Caucasus. Russia faces a dilemma: It fears the power of Islam as a potential anti-Russian factor in the region and at the same time seeks to play a major role in the Muslim world, including the Middle East. The Russian-Muslim cultural borders thus present complex and highly unresolved problems, with a legacy of two-way imperialism and expansionism. They will particularly bear watching as both Russia and its new Muslim neighbors move into unexplored phases of postimperial bilateral relations.

If the geopolitics of the past are any indication, cultural rivalry between the two huge cultural blocs of Christian, Orthodox Slavic Russia and the Muslim Turkic lands, including Turkey, can easily reemerge as each center seeks economic, political, and cultural dominance in the Caucasus and Central Asia. And today's Central Asia is a far more weighty Islamic cultural entity, now defined much more broadly than in the period of the Soviet Empire. Today it includes once again Iran, Afghanistan, and Pakistan as part of the Central Asian equation vis-à-vis Russia.

China

China's borders with Central Asia also represent a potential flashpoint with Islam, even though China is not Christian. China has an ethnic Turkic Muslim population—the Uighur Turks—of some 8 million people in western China, the historic Chinese Turkestan. They are closely linked culturally to the Uzbeks over the border in the former Soviet Union. They have suffered for many years from "ethnic cleansing" and demographic pressures from the forced settlement of Han Chinese into the region to weaken Uighur ethnic unity and to assimilate them. Uighurs aspire to far greater autonomy, if not independence, from China. As the Chinese Communist regime in Beijing weakens, separatist tendencies in Chinese Turkestan grow, paralleling similar aspirations in neighboring Tibet. Serious conflict is quite possible if the Uighurs engage in an independence struggle. In Chinese Turkestan the fundamental issue is not Islam at all but a national liberation movement parallel to the Buddhist Tibetans and Mongols. Already present as a factor, Islam will inevitably grow to strengthen the Uighur nationalist identity, as yet another cultural feature distinguishing them from the Han Chinese.

The Uighurs are not even the biggest Muslim group in China. There are over 10 million Hui Muslims, who speak Chinese as their native language and are often scarcely distinguishable from Han Chinese in appearance, dress, and many customs, yet who clearly see themselves as a distinct ethnic group and nationality within China based on religion.[3] Their communities are scattered throughout China, but the greatest number are found in Ningxia Province in the north-central part of the Chinese state. The Hui are likely to increasingly insist on their rights as a minority nationality, even though secession is not a realistic goal. As nationality issues in China grow more open and active, the Hui will be a highly self-conscious group interested in expanding their contacts with other Muslim communities worldwide. So far historically they have not been close to the Uighurs, whom they regard as a distinctly different ethnic group. The fall of the communist regime in Beijing would raise questions about how the Hui people will seek to place themselves in a new political environment. The likelihood of greater Islamic solidarity increases as their chances for external contacts grow. In this region, then, Islam is separatist in character and will be involved in a struggle for territory, especially territory that contains rich oil deposits. Resentment of past Han imperial control is also a potent factor.

The Indian Subcontinent

Islam in the Indian subcontinent no longer adjoins the West or the Christian world; it interacts with the Hindu world. Nonetheless, for Islam it is a cultural border of considerable tension, with direct impact on Islam's broader world outlook. Some Hindu political parties within India implicitly and explicitly talk of cooperation with the West against the "Islamic threat."

The history of the Indian subcontinent also reveals features of role reversal in power relationships between Muslims and Hindus. India was ruled by a brilliant Muslim dynasty, the Mughals, from the beginning of the seventeenth century until the British took over India in the early nineteenth century. The Mughals were originally Turkic in origin and came directly out of Central Asia via Afghanistan to conquer and rule India from Delhi, creating a dynasty that was one of the highpoints of Indian cultural development. A minority Muslim population thus ruled over a Hindu majority for centuries only to have the roles reversed as British rule gradually accorded greater power to Hindu institutions, culminating in the eventual dominance of the Hindus after independence in 1947. Some autonomous Muslim princely states such as Hyderabad existed intact within India until independence.

Muslims thus had a profound sense of loss of place and power. Their proportional demographic weight in India was then vastly reduced with the creation of a breakaway Muslim state, West Pakistan and East Pakistan (today's Bangladesh), and the emigration of a large number of Indian Muslims to Pakistan and Bangladesh. Today Muslims represent no more than 12 percent of the Indian population—a massive drop in their relative proportion of the population before the partition of India. Communal tensions remain high. India's Congress Party has sought to give the Muslims special cultural concessions in return for their long-term loyalty to the party, while Hindu nationalist parties have grown angry at those concessions and seek to Hinduize the entire country. Over 40 years of hostility between Muslim Pakistan and largely Hindu India have further strained relations, sometimes even calling into question the loyalty of India's Muslims in Indo-Pakistani conflicts. Differences are mainly religious, for Indian Muslims otherwise share intimately with Hindus common culture, food, music, and even language to a considerable extent. No clear-cut ethnic differences remain apart from religion.

Power relationships between the two communities are also at the center of the conflict. Over 100 million Indian Muslims (the second largest Muslim community in the world) are destined to live as a permanent minority in

India because there is no remote chance for them either to break away or to declare an autonomous region inside the country because they are a highly scattered population. Because of Islam's stress on the *religious* importance of maintaining a consolidated community under the rule of Muslims, this kind of minority status for Indian Muslims in an overwhelmingly Hindu state is particularly painful. The growth of powerful Hindu nationalist and even chauvinist parties in India raises the prospect for greater internal conflict and bloodshed, with no solution, however radical, in sight other than gradually acquired common sense and coexistence on both sides. India is one of the few states in the world where such a large Muslim population has no other options except emigration.

The Indian state of Jammu-Kashmir, with its predominant Muslim majority, is the only significant area where the potential of separatism is realistic and high. The Muslim rebellion (or *intifada*) in Kashmir is growing, based on deep Kashmiri grievances and fueled by Pakistani support and ruthless, unenlightened security measures by the Indian state against the population as a whole. Consistent refusal by India to permit any UN-mandated plebiscite in the area has been at the heart of the Indo-Pakistani quarrel for decades. In a plebiscite today Muslim Kashmir would almost surely vote for outright independence from India, but not necessarily for subsequent unification with Pakistan. The issue is highly volatile and has been a key cause of past Indo-Pakistani wars. Most Indians see retention of Kashmir, even by force, as a non-negotiable matter of principle and essential to the preservation of the multiethnic Indian state as a whole. Thus Muslim separatism is also a factor in India, although only in Kashmir.

India established diplomatic relations with Israel in 1992 and has publicly spoken of cooperation with Israel against Islamic fundamentalism. India is equally concerned about the emergence of five new independent Muslim countries in nearby Central Asia that strengthens the "Islamic strategic depth" of Pakistan, replacing the Soviet-dominated, officially pro-India, non-religious Central Asia of the past. Although the Central Asian states seek good relations with India, Delhi is nonetheless worried about the potential growth of fundamentalism there and the growing role of other Islamic countries in Central Asian politics and economics.

In short, the Indian subcontinent possesses significant flashpoints for Islam in the future that cannot be completely divorced from Islam's problems in the West. The chief difference is that Hinduism, rather than Christianity, is Islam's main challenger and, in Muslim eyes, oppressor. The problems are territorial (Kashmir), religious (preservation of the Islamic community and its religious privileges in India), political-psychological (the legacy of former Muslim dominance and the subsequent Hindu dominance over Muslims), and military (India versus Pakistan).

Southeast Asia

Islam came rather later to Southeast Asia. Its main strength is in Indonesia, which has the largest Muslim population in the world, and in Malaysia, whose population is half Muslim. Smaller Muslim populations exist in southern Thailand and in the Philippines. Indonesia has had a tradition of largely secular government since independence, and the country's leadership has sought to foster a secular nationalist-ethical ideology, Pancsila, as a means of fusing the diverse populations of the country into one nationalist whole. Although this ideology has been far less militantly secular than the Ataturkist movement in Turkey, there has long been a latent tension between it, perceived as a "government ideology," and the more orthodox Islamic tendencies, including Islamist movements. Islamists, and undoubtedly many elements of the population, are resentful that the Muslim majority (85 percent) of the country has been required to give up Islam as the national religion out of deference to non-Muslim minorities. Hence there is some agitation for abandonment of Pancsila in favor of Islam. This poses a critical test for the future of Indonesian secularism. As elsewhere in the Muslim world, the strains of modernization and powerful Western cultural infiltration have caused the kind of psychological and cultural dislocations and malaise that encourage the growth of Islamist movements elsewhere. External influences from Libya, Saudi Arabia, and Iran have also had modest impact. Finally, Indonesians have felt pride in association with the rising power of Muslim oil states and seek a greater voice for Muslim states in international affairs. Thus solid grounds exist for the continued growth of Muslim solidarity, even though Indonesians do not identify with most of the chaotic, confrontational politics of the Arab world and feel themselves to be quite politically distinct with their own geopolitical interests.[4]

With only half of its population Muslim and Malay, Malaysia is quite sensitive to religious and ethnic fault lines within its multiethnic and multireligious society. Malaysian economic success will help to soften these potential cultural confrontations, which include considerable disparity in economic position, particularly between a Chinese merchant class and the Malay population. It is interesting to note that Malaysia becomes a possible point of confluence for Confucian and Islamic critiques of Western culture and its ethical and social weaknesses. Prime Minister Mahathir has been an outspoken critic of Western cultural domination, less along Islamist lines than lines parallel to many of the sharp critiques leveled at the West by his neighbor President Lee Kuan Yew of Singapore and Lee's foreign minister.

Thus general sources of conflict in Southeast Asia between Islam and non-Islam involve internal competition between Muslim and non-Muslim populations. These are most often expressed in ethnic rather than religious terms and spring from a perceived need for a strong cultural front against the economic and cultural strength of Chinese and Hindu communities. Muslim separatist aspirations exist in Thailand and the Philippines, and Islam is readily impressed into service as the cultural vehicle in this rivalry. Tensions with the West in Southeast Asia are less urgent than in the western Muslim world, but they are clearly present in resentment of Western dominance of international political, cultural, and economic institutions.

Although radical Islam is less deeply developed in Southeast Asia than in the western Muslim world, it does share many of the same roots, despite cultural differences. It is very likely to develop more significant strength in the years ahead, even if unable to come to power by the ballot box. Its growth, as elsewhere, will be contingent upon the ability of governments to meet the economic, social, and psychological needs of the population in times of rapid and dislocating change.

Africa

Africa today is one of the more volatile borders between Islam and the non-Muslim world. First, whereas Islam accords Christianity and Judaism full religious respect, it has no respect for animist religions and views those communities as prime areas for conversion to Islam. Islam has thus been steadily moving south into sub-Saharan Africa. A state such as Sudan is itself split between a Muslim north and an animist and partially Christian south; an ugly civil war has been raging between the two regions off and on since Sudanese independence in 1956, and the present Islamist regime seeks to "Islamize" and "Arabize" the south entirely. These two trends of Islamization and Arabization are very old and were the vehicles that brought Islam to Sudan in the first place many hundreds of years ago: Not by conquest but through proselytization by merchant and religious brotherhoods did Islam take hold in Africa. Indeed, brotherhood activity runs deep in the African tradition of Islam, right across North Africa and south from there. Libyan orders have long participated in extending Islam southwards, as have those in Morocco.

The southern extension of Islam obviously includes expansion of political influence not welcomed by most African states. Islam is invariably involved in the local contest for power as well. Nigeria, divided between Christian and Muslim regions, is involved in a struggle of this sort; many Nigerian Islamists seek to turn Nigeria into an Islamist state and have received encouragement from Iran and Saudi Arabia.[5] Civil strife over these issues is likely to grow. Uganda is also affected in similar ways. Ethiopia has managed its Christian-Muslim relations far better, but the issue is unresolved and will undoubtedly remain a target of Islamist activists. Clashes along this fault line may be some of the most intense in the coming decades, especially as Africa begins the process of sorting out differences between borders and ethnicity, an issue it has deliberately avoided for decades after independence. Islam is likely to be a significant factor in what will be a broader issue of separatism throughout the continent. In most cases Islam per se is not the basis of separatism so much as ethnic differences reinforced by religious identity.

In Africa, then, issues of struggle for internal power, separatism, and prose-lytization characterize the Islamic fault line. Islamic proselytization is a far more prominent factor in Africa than in any other part of the world. Islam's social and cultural power will likely give Muslim communities considerable weight in future ethnic-cultural struggles on the continent, especially in relation to non-Muslim communities that are, in many cases, local and weaker in social structure.

North America

Islam has shown dramatic growth in North America over the past several decades, where it is becoming the second largest faith after Christianity. Its growth results from the immigration of large numbers of Muslims as well as the conversion of African Americans into black Muslim organizations. Among African Americans, the Nation of Islam movement, while quite openly anti-Semitic and racist, has also provided a striking source of social discipline in poor communities where family structures have crumbled.

The Islam of Muslim immigrants to the United States is likely to seek accommodation with mainstream American culture and to be somewhat secularized by the experience (see the earlier discussion of dilemmas posed by the West to the Islamic world). The role of Islam among African Americans, however, is probably much more dynamic; it is in competition with the powerful social institutions of Christian churches and is also linked to a broader alternative tendency toward separatism found among African Americans in recent years. This controversial aspect of North American Islam has become linked via the very recently arrived Islamic movement to the broader social, political, and economic tensions within American society—with unpredictable paths still ahead.

Islam's global fault lines, then, are many and varied, adjoining two major strains of Christianity as well as Buddhist, Hindu, and Confucian cultures. Islam as a religion is not the source of conflict, but in a world of increasingly diverse ethnic and religious frictions, Islam will be invoked as a factor—in most cases combined with ethnicity. The strong international cultural bonds of Islam will lend it a capacity for international solidarity beyond that of other world religions. This associational strength can be, and will be, intimidating to groups whose numbers and sense of communal solidarity are less pronounced.

Notes

1. Huntington, "The Clash of Civilizations?", p. 35.

2. When confronted with this reality, Muslims nonetheless often counter by saying that Western *populations* may have sympathy for the Bosnian Muslims, but they and their governments are still sufficiently unmoved to actually do anything about it.

3. See Dru C. Gladney, *Muslim Chinese: Ethnic Nationalism in the People's Republic* (Cambridge, MA: Harvard University Press, 1991), p. viii.

4. Anthony H. Johns, "Indonesia: Islam and Cultural Pluralism," in John L. Esposito, ed., *Islam in Asia: Religion, Politics and Society,* pp. 223–228 (New York: Oxford University Press, 1987). Also see Fred R. von der Mehden., "Indonesia and Malaysia," in Shireen T. Hunter, ed., *The Politics of Islamic Revivalism* (Bloomington: Indiana University Press, 1987).

5. John Hunwick, "An African Case Study of Political Islam," *Annals of the American Academy of Political and Social Science,* November 1992.

9

THE STRATEGIC DIMENSION

The future character of relations between Islam and the West will influence the propensity for conflict in the international system, and will pose new challenges for Western policy and strategy. Key issues in this context include the interaction of differing strategic cultures and attitudes toward war and peace; the special role of states on the borderlands between Islam and the West; the implications for stability and deterrence of an environment in which the Islamic factor is more prominent in security terms; and the pressures for and consequences of Western military intervention in the Third World and the Muslim world in particular.

A Clash of Strategic Cultures?

As strategists and policy makers consider the implications of the end of the Cold War for established approaches to the use of force and concepts of security, it will be especially important to recognize the danger of ethnocentrism in strategic assessments. The prevailing strategic lexicon, from notions of polarity to deterrence, is part of the Western intellectual tradition. Leaderships in the Muslim world have no doubt incorporated a great deal of the Western approach to thinking about international conflict, just as over time Soviet strategists came to adopt an essentially U.S. approach to thinking about strategic stability. Over centuries of interaction and retrenchment the Islamic strategic view evolved from what might have been described as a "world domination theory" to a more circumscribed one, fashioned within the constraints imposed by a Western-dominated order.[1]

Modern Western thinking about warfare and strategy has been dominated by the Clausewitzian notion of a close connection between war and politics. But as one noted military historian has reminded us, culture too is a prime determinant of the nature of warfare, in some instances perhaps a dominant one.[2] Despite the general perception of Islam as a religion of conquest and holy war, study of the practice of warfare within the Muslim tradition reveals a strong preference for restraint in warfare, including reliance on symbolism and the indirect approach.[3] In fact, the emblematic era of rapid Muslim conquest was short and was followed by a far longer period in which warfare and military organization became more and more the province of a warrior class recruited from the borderlands of Islam. The obligation of *jihad,* as well as strictures against conflict within the Islamic community lost much of their original force. Indeed, Islam's strategic retrenchment along the European periphery from the end of the fourteenth century onward was in large measure the result of encountering the full force of another strategic tradition, the Western, "which recognized none of the constraints the Oriental tradition had imposed upon itself."[4] At the same time the Islamic tradition itself had a marked impact on Western strategic culture beginning with the experience of the Crusades:

> There was . . . a cultural exchange of great importance that resulted from the conflict of Muslim and Christian in the Middle East. The conflict resolved the inherent Christian dilemma over the reality of warmaking by transmitting to the West the ethic of holy war, which was thereafter to invest Western military culture with an ideological and intellectual dimension it had hitherto lacked.[5]

Yet even allowing for the fact that Muslim culture has favored a relatively constrained and often indirect approach to war-making at the operational level, Islam has been and remains "the most martial of the world's great religions." This is the practical legacy of the Muslim and Ottoman traditions in which warfare played an integral role "precisely because it served religious, political and legal ends."[6] Religious imagery continues to play a more central role in Muslim thought and practice in times of conflict than it does in Western society. As an example, the use of religious imagery to describe war aims was present, especially on the Iranian side in the Iran-Iraq War. But in the context of conflict between Muslims and non-Muslims, not surprisingly, that Islam itself emerges as a powerful force. In the 1973 Arab-Israeli War and in the 1974 conflict between Turkey and Greece over Cyprus the language and the rhetoric accompanying the fighting was strikingly religious.[7] The latter case is especially noteworthy, since the Turkish military is the most avowedly secular component of an overtly secular Muslim society. Throughout the Muslim world Islam itself is a powerful point of reference in times of tension and conflict. By contrast, notions of *jihad,* or holy war, no longer have any correlate in the secular strategic tradition of the West.

Most scholarship with regard to Islamic strategic culture focuses on concepts of just war (*jus ad bellum*), and even here there is no strong consensus: "One cannot identify a single classical theory of Islam in relation to war." Some broadly accepted categories of justifiable war in the Islamic tradition include obligations to "eliminate repression, ensure the free observance of religion, defend Islamic territories against foreign aggression, and uphold the authority of the Islamic state against armed rebellion."[8] On the conduct of war itself (*jus in bello*), including questions of proportionality, attacks on civilians, and damage to economic infrastructure, Muslim theory on the whole has less to say than comparable religious, legal, and strategic traditions in the West.[9]

The proper question is not whether Islam per se is any more warlike than other traditions. Rather, it is whether religious extremism of any sort increases the propensity to use force as a means of altering the international environment.[10] There is, of course, a risk that Islam may be selectively interpreted by leaderships to mobilize their populations for war (Saddam Hussein pursued this with limited success in the Gulf crisis).[11] Another approach, valid in the more generic context of North-South frictions, might be the distinction between status quo and revolutionary regimes—haves and have-nots—noted earlier. What is most disturbing about radical Islam from a strategic perspective may well be the potentially explosive interaction of transcendent religious fervor with "revolutionary" international aims. If correct, this would imply a structural conflict between "fundamentalist" Islam and the West, with little prospect of mutual accommodation. This point takes on added significance in light of the tendency of military officers in Muslim states to talk in terms of their commitment to radical change in domestic and international politics.[12] This phenomenon, of which there have been many notable examples in the modern Middle East (e.g., Nasser, Saddam Hussein, Qadhafi, in a very different sense even Ataturk), is in strong contrast to the Western tradition in which military officers are more typically associated with conservative rather than revolutionary attitudes.

The experience of Afghanistan and the Gulf War has been central to the strategic outlook of contemporary Islamists as well as military establishments in the Muslim world. The former proved the ability of Islamic forces to defeat a ("atheistic") superpower in its own backyard. If one accepts the argument that the Soviet defeat in Afghanistan hastened the disintegration of the Soviet Union itself, the Islamist victory appears even more profound. In this context the prestige and influence of Afghan veterans in Algeria and Egypt is hardly surprising. From the Gulf experience many Islamists have drawn the conclusion that the West is now more willing to intervene in the Muslim world than it was during the Cold War, and that these interventions are likely to be characterized by the defense of rich regimes against the poor.[13] Furthermore, the willingness of prominent regimes in the Muslim world to join in the Western coalition against Saddam Hussein has contributed to the Islamist critique of existing regimes as illegitimate and dependent on Western support for their political survival.

In many respects Muslim attitudes toward the use of force are a product not only of religious tradition but also of the circumstances confronting contemporary Muslim states. These are, for the most part, insecure societies facing serious internal and external challenges. The appeal of transcendent principles, whether they flow from religion or political ideology, is bound to be more powerful under these conditions. As elsewhere in the Third World, force is not perceived as having lost its utility in reshaping either the internal or the external environment. Sensitivity to military and civilian casualties, while hardly absent, is not as pronounced as in the United States or Europe.[14] Muslim perceptions of external security problems are frequently tied to internal vulnerabilities and the fear that these may be exploited: thus the extraordinary Algerian, Egyptian, Tunisian, and Turkish concern with alleged Iranian and Sudanese attempts at destabilization. The West may loom as a convenient enemy (sometimes, as in the case of Libya or Iran, the United States is a leading adversary), but the real security concerns are usually closer to home—regional rivals or internal threats to the legitimacy and power of existing regimes. The content of security policy in Muslim states is overwhelmingly internal or regional, with "over the horizon" objectives a generally distant third.

Deterrence and Extended Deterrence

Differences in strategic culture between Islam and the West could introduce enormous uncertainties in the deterrent calculus that strategists and policy makers used to Cold War assumptions have only begun to ponder. As long as the states of the Muslim periphery are unable to bring their military power to bear directly on Western territory, questions of deterrence outside the traditional east-west context receive justifiably little attention (except in considering responses to Western intervention in the Gulf or elsewhere). The spread of weapons of mass destruction and the means for their delivery at increasing ranges suggest that this period of sanctuarization from retaliation and strategic blackmail is drawing to a end. In the future, deterrence in Europe (and for the United States and NATO, extended deterrence) is likely to be a broad, multiregional issue. The proliferation of ballistic missiles with ranges upward of 1,000 km along the southern and eastern shores of the Mediterranean will place all of NATO's southern allies at risk. With growing missile accuracy U.S. military forces in the region will also be exposed to attack. Unless coupled with nuclear weapons, the military significance of threats from this quarter is likely to be limited, but the political significance for U.S. bilateral and NATO relations would be substantial. Proliferation trends are bringing the Muslim Middle Eastern and European security environments closer together in a way that was only hinted at in the Gulf War.

European exposure to long-range arsenals in the Muslim south could alter the calculus of security cooperation in future crises. Countries such as Spain, Italy, and Greece would undoubtedly confront a more serious domestic debate over the risks of cooperation and the possibility of retaliation. It is most likely that policy makers in southern Europe would still agree to provide the United States with access to bases and overflight rights and might still provide forces of their own for operations in North Africa or the Gulf, but Allied expectations with regard to air and ballistic missile defense would certainly increase. The extent to which a Western intervention somewhere in the Middle East could escalate to a more general military confrontation between Islam and the West cannot be predicted in general terms. The stakes and potential for unified action are too dependent on the character of specific cases and domestic factors discussed earlier. But the Gulf experience highlights some of the risks. Even with the substantial involvement of leading Arab states in the coalition of forces ranged against Iraq, opinion across the Muslim world, not least in North Africa, was highly critical of Western policy. Indeed, public support for Saddam Hussein was, and remains, widespread across North Africa, with notable emphasis on his rather peculiar and recently acquired status as a defender of Muslim interests against an aggressive West. The potential for Islamic political solidarity of this sort to evolve into a more unified military stance is limited, but the pressures for this union in times of crisis may well expand as Europe's Islamic periphery acquires a more credible capacity for response and as Islamic politics acquire greater importance throughout the Middle East.

In the emerging strategic environment, considerations of deterrence and extended deterrence will, de facto, have a strong Western-Muslim presence as a consequence of instability in the Greater Middle East, frictions along the borderlands with Islam, and the spread of weapons of mass destruction in

these same regions.[15] Western military forces will also play a role in the
strategic reassurance of countries within the Muslim world against threats to
their own territory and stability. Setting aside Turkish concerns about the
solidity of the NATO guarantee in Middle Eastern contingencies, there can be
little doubt that Ankara's Western security ties will continue to figure prominently in the deterrence of Iran, Iraq, and Syria. In a less formal sense the
likelihood of European and U.S. intervention will remain an important part
of the strategic calculus between Morocco and Algeria, Tunisia and Libya,
and Egypt vis à vis Libya and Sudan. Above all, and for the foreseeable
future, the United States is likely to remain the principal security guarantor
for the oil-producing kingdoms of the Persian Gulf. Taking all these relationships into account, it is clear that new thinking about deterrence in a
post–Cold War setting will require a much deeper understanding of strategic
thought and practice in the Muslim world than was necessary when "trip-
wire" and over-the-horizon postures were framed with reference to a Soviet
threat. The experience of the Gulf War provided a striking example of
Western "difficulty in coming to grips with a political and cultural system as
alien as that of Baathist Iraq." Even at the operational level Western comman-
ders proceeded against Iraqi forces as if they were "Soviets who spoke
Arabic," a natural result of decades of Cold War planning and unfamiliarity
with an adversary whose weapons were recognizable but whose strategic
outlook was alien.[16]

Borderlands Revisited

In his much-debated *Foreign Affairs* article, Samuel Huntington has made
reference to "Islam's bloody borders" as mentioned earlier. In a literal sense
his observation is correct, as conflicts along religious lines from the Balkans
to South and Central Asia and beyond demonstrate. But the impression that
Islam is incapable of peaceful coexistence where civilizations meet is misleading. Like much of the Third World, the Muslim world is indeed prone to
political violence and conflict, but these patterns of behavior are oriented
overwhelmingly along Muslim-Muslim rather than Muslim-Western lines.
Even where Islam and other civilizations are in conflict, Muslims are just as
likely to see themselves as the culture under siege. Huntington's formulation
is, above all, a reflection on the tendency of turmoil within the Muslim world
to overflow its borders and affect the security of neighboring, non-Muslim
societies. In the new strategic environment on Europe's periphery, states on

the borderlands between Muslim and Western civilizations have acquired renewed importance as a consequence of their exposure to conflict and their potential as interlocutors. This situation is in direct contrast to that of the Cold War, in which states on the European and Asian marches were relegated to the political and strategic, as well as geographic, periphery. The border-lands between Islam and the West derive additional significance in the new environment as places where historical images of relations between the two civilizations are most firmly entrenched and enduring.

Within the West the countries of southern Europe are most exposed to the challenges of proliferation, migration, and instability in the Muslim south.[17] Spain and Greece are the two countries of the European Union whose relations with the Muslim world include potentially inflammatory disputes over populations and territory. It would be difficult for Europe and the United States to stand aside from a clash between Madrid and Rabat over disputed Spanish enclaves of Ceuta and Melilla opposite Gibraltar, which regardless of any other effects would threaten shipping through the world's busiest water-way. Similarly, renewed hostilities between Ankara and Athens over Cyprus, the use of the Aegean or wider Balkan issues, would present the most serious dilemmas for Washington and the Atlantic Alliance. In this context France, too, is very much a *marca* or borderland state, with a considerable southern exposure and stake in the evolution of the Mediterranean region in security terms. Together with Spain and Italy, France is likely to be an increasingly essential partner for the United States in managing relations with the Islamic world.[18]

The reorientation of U.S. national security strategy toward regional contingencies—many of which are likely to arise from instability in the Muslim world—could benefit substantially from the experience and position of key borderland states in southern Europe. As one observer has noted, "An exit from this predicament [of strategic reorientation] is best prepared by cooperating closely with the European Community and by accepting Southern Europe's *marca* states as lead actors in the confrontation with Islam."[19] "Confrontation" may be the wrong term to describe a relationship that cannot be characterized as a bloc-to-bloc conflict, but the broad point about new partners in relations with the Muslim world still holds. France, in particular, is seen to have a great deal to offer in the area of strategic intelligence, oriented southward.[20]

Moreover, the value of the borderland states is not limited to the confrontational aspects of relations with Muslim states. The prospects for greater political, economic, and military cooperation across civilizational lines will also depend to a great extent on policies adopted in Paris, Madrid, and Rome. Through their own diplomatic initiatives, the European countries of the western Mediterranean have emerged as the leading advocates of North-South diplomacy in the region.[21] In a more tangible sense they are also the architects of the European Community's revitalized Mediterranean policy, conduits for investment and development assistance, and participants in arms and technology transfers as well as new energy schemes.

Islam's *marca* states will play an equally important role in this regard. Morocco and Turkey, in different ways, provide excellent examples. Despite lingering concerns over human rights and the slow pace of political reform, the European Union has turned to Morocco as the focus for its policy toward North Africa as a whole. King Hassan, for his part, has been very active in projecting an image of the country as a valuable interlocutor between North and South, Islam and the West.[22] His role in the recent Israeli-Palestinian negotiations provides a useful example of this. At the opposite end of the Mediterranean Turkey views its role as that of a bridge between civilizations in strategic as well as political and cultural terms. Ankara has not been as successful as it might wish in developing its role as a bridge—as noted earlier, the requisite interest in Turkey as an interlocutor is often missing in both Europe and the Muslim world, and its security role is more akin to a barrier—but the aspiration and the potential remain. Turkey can indeed play an important role in the development and security of areas as diverse as the Balkans, the Caucasus, and Central Asia. Above all, Turkey's position as a *marca* state par excellence makes the evolution of its foreign and security policies increasingly important to the Muslim world and to the West.

As has been observed, Turkey is itself torn between its Islamic and Western vocations. As the secular, Western-oriented Ataturkist tradition comes under pressure from many quarters, developments in Bosnia and the Caucasus have introduced new tensions in Ankara's external relations. These may have a direct effect on U.S. policy, as in the overt linkage between Turkish cooperation on Iraq and Western action on Bosnia. To the extent that cleavages between Islam and the West become more prominent in security terms, the Turkish predicament will deepen, and Ankara may become a more difficult and less predictable partner for the West. Turks will be reluctant to cooperate in policies that may be seen as anti-Islam. At the same time Europe will be increasingly reluctant to accept an automatic responsibility for the security of a country whose interests, in their view, lie elsewhere—in the Muslim world. The evolution of security relations along these lines would be disastrous for Turkey and would severely limit the prospects for U.S.-Turkish cooperation and, by extension, U.S. freedom of action in the Caucasus and the Middle East.

Western interest in the evolution of Russian policy is also likely to have a strong "southern" component, extending outward to Central Asia. Indeed, our interest in Moscow's behavior and presence along its southern borders with Islam may rival or even outstrip concerns about the evolution of the country's relations in central and Eastern Europe. Certainly this is an area in which policy is relatively fluid and, in contrast to relations on Russia's European borders, strategic stakes and perceptions are ill-formed.

In contrast to the trend in grand strategic thinking during the Cold War, many of the strategic "prizes" in the new environment are likely to be found on the periphery, where religions and cultures meet and the risk of conflict is greatest. To the extent that U.S. and European foreign policies aim to enhance stability in regions of vital interest, developments and relationships on the borderlands between Islam and other cultures should be of far greater importance than at any time in the recent past. Beyond direct security problems, this implies at least as much concern for the long-term political and economic development of key states such as Egypt and Turkey as for the future of former communist regimes in Eastern Europe. The systemic and regional risks associated with the failure of societies in the Muslim world, although different in texture, are just as serious for the security of the West.

Islam, Third World Conflict, and Western Intervention

Despite the intense discussion of cleavages and flashpoints between Islam and the West, the risk of direct conflict in the new strategic environment is concentrated largely within the Muslim world itself, along South-South rather than North-South lines. The most dangerous flashpoints are within, rather than between, civilizations. This too will have important consequences for Western policy. The proliferation of weapons of mass destruction in the Middle East affects the security of Europe and the freedom of action of the United States despite the fact that the primary impetus for acquiring these weapons is regional rather than global. The insecure nature of Muslim societies and the prevalence of regional rivalries within the Muslim world (these are, in fact, characteristics of the Third World more generally) will also affect the frequency and nature of Western intervention in the post–Cold War world.[23]

Of 13 current UN peacekeeping operations, 9 are either in Muslim countries or involve Muslim interests directly: the Sinai (since 1967, but following on from operations since 1948); India-Pakistan (Kashmir, since 1949); Cyprus (since 1964); Golan Heights (since 1974); Lebanon (since 1978); Iraq-Kuwait (since 1991); Western Sahara (since 1991); the former Yugoslavia (since 1992); Somalia (since 1992). These operations represent roughly two-thirds of the total troop and police strength deployed under UN auspices.

If peacekeeping is to be an important thrust of future U.S. and European strategy and force planning, it is difficult to escape the conclusion that this will necessarily bring U.S. policy makers and U.S. forces into closer contact with Muslim interests and populations. This is likely to be true regardless of whether U.S. forces are involved "on the ground." As a preeminent actor in the United Nations, Washington plays a major role in decisions related to peacekeeping and peace enforcement. Its decisions will be the subject of keen interest across the Muslim world. In the context of peacekeeping and "peacemaking" operations, the United Nations has already emerged as a key forum for the legitimation of military action. Freed of Cold War alignments, it could also emerge as an important forum for the articulation of Muslim and broader Third World interests.[24] The result could well be heightened friction between an outspoken Muslim bloc within the United Nations and the non-Muslim principals in the Security Council (and Western security organizations such as NATO and the Western European Union that would very likely be the executors for peacekeeping and peacemaking operations of any size). Having said this, the demand for Muslim peacekeeping forces is likely to be substantial, with countries such as Turkey, Pakistan, and Egypt well situated to play a leading role in those cases where cultural and political factors are paramount.[25] Indeed, it would be surprising if this reality did not eventually lead to serious consideration of some form of permanent, perhaps rotating, Muslim presence on the UN Security Council.

Overall, the confluence of instability within the Muslim world and a growing emphasis on peacekeeping in the West argues for very careful diplomacy within international organizations, and sensitive handling of command arrangements in peacekeeping operations. Since the intelligence-gathering, logistical, and command and control capabilities necessary for effective operations of any scale reside in Western (above all, U.S.) military establishments, peacekeeping in the Muslim world cannot easily be left to Muslim states. In some cases it may be appropriate to envision a substantial role for Muslim forces "on the ground," with Western forces in a supporting role over the horizon.

Notes

1. See Ken Booth, *Strategy and Ethnocentrism* (London: Croom Helm, 1979), p. 76; and Majid Khadduri, *War and Peace in the Law of Islam* (Baltimore: Johns Hopkins University Press, 1955).

2. John Keegan, *A History of Warfare* (New York: Alfred A. Knopf, 1993).

3. See V. J. Parry and M. E. Yapp (eds.), *War, Technology and Society in the Middle East* (London: Oxford University Press, 1975).

4. Keegan, *A History of Warfare*, p. 389.

5. Ibid., p. 390.

6. Dankwart A. Rustow, "Political Ends and Military Means in the late-Ottoman and post-Ottoman Middle East," in Parry and Yapp, *War, Technology and Society in the Middle East*, p. 387.

7. Lewis, *Islam and the West*, p. 152.

8. David R. Smock, *Religious Perspectives on War: Christian, Muslim and Jewish Attitudes toward Force after the Gulf War* (Washington, D.C.: U.S. Institute of Peace, 1992), pp. 26–27.

9. See ibid.; and James T. Johnson and John Kelsay, eds., *Cross, Crescent and Sword: The Justification and Limitation of War in Western and Islamic Traditions* (New York: Greenwood Press, 1990).

10. This question is assessed in relation to terrorist movements in Bruce Hoffman, "Holy Terror: The Implications of Terrorism Motivated by a Religious Imperative," paper presented at conference, "Worldwide Department of Defense Combatting Terrorism," Virginia Beach, VA, June 8–11, 1993; reprinted as P-7834 (Santa Monica, CA: RAND, 1994).

11. David, "Why the Third World Still Matters," p. 137.

12. See Morris Janowitz, "Some Observations on the Comparative Analysis of Middle Eastern Military Institutions," in Parry and Yapp, *War, Technology and Society in the Middle East*.

13. Salame, "Islam and the West," p.28.

14. The costly offensive tactics employed by both sides against strong defensive positions in the Iran-Iraq War would have appalled Europeans who have not forgotten images of Verdun and the Somme.

15. See Colonel Qadhafi's comments on deterrence, *FBIS-NES,* October 1, 1992, p. 9.

16. Eliot A. Cohen, "Tales of the Desert: Searching for Context for the Persian Gulf War (Review Essay)," Foreign Affairs, May/June 1994, p. 145.

17. These issues are examined from both a southern European and North African perspective in Vasconcelos, *Européens et Maghrébins.*

18. In addition to the French contribution in the Gulf and a central role in UN peacekeeping in Bosnia, France is the most likely partner for any intervention or peacekeeping operations in North Africa. At the time of the January 1980 Gafsa incident, France sent naval forces to the Tunisian coast to forestall further Libyan aggression. See Richard B. Parker, *North Africa: Regional Tensions and Strategic Concerns* (New York: Council on Foreign Relations, 1987); on Spanish and other European contributions during the Gulf War, see Nicole Gnesotto and John Roper, eds., *Western Europe and the Gulf* (Paris: Western European Union Institute for Security Studies, 1992).

19. Bozeman, *Strategic Intelligence and Statecraft,* p. 354.

20. French strategic perceptions are discussed in Marc Bonnefous. "Politique et Strategie au Sud," *Defense Nationale,* May 1993.

21. See Vasconcelos, *Européens et Maghrébins;* and Alejandro Lorca and Jesús Nuñez, "The Economy of the Maghreb: Reality and Hope," paper prepared for international conference, "The Mediterranean: Risks and Challenges," IAI, Rome, November 27–28, 1992.

22. See "King Hassan on Relations with Arab East, EC," *FBIS-NES,* January 14, 1992, pp. 13–14.

23. On war as a Third World phenomenon see Guy Arnold, *Wars in the Third World since 1945* (London: Cassell, 1991).

24. See Bruce Russett, *A Post-Thucydides, Post–Cold War World* (Athens: Institute of International Relations, Panteion University, 1992), pp. 6–7.

25. As in Somalia, where the UN forces, including U.S. troops, are under the command of a Turkish general and Pakistani soldiers are present in large numbers.

10

CONCLUSIONS

We do not believe that relations between Islam and the West per se represent the arena of "the next global ideological struggle." Despite historic rivalry as the only two world claimants to be "universal faiths," Islam as a *religion* today is not on a collision course with Christianity or the West. Moreover, we do not foresee broad confrontation between an Islamic bloc and a Western bloc of states as in any way inevitable. The countries, situations, and interests involved are simply too diverse and varied to sustain major long-term polarization of cultural-religious blocs.

Salience of the Islamic Factor

Nonetheless, gross mishandling of political relationships on both sides can intensify the *ideological,* as opposed to practical, element in situations of Muslim-Western friction or confrontation and could even lead to a transient ideological consolidation of numerous Muslim states. The Islamic factor is likely to become an increasingly prominent aspect of strategic and geopolitical focus between the Muslim world and the West in the decade ahead. This is because Islam is increasingly used as a kind of political shorthand—wrongly we believe—to describe societal, political, cultural, economic, and strategic differences between North and South. Several elements will give salience to the Islamic factor in relations between Islam and the West. First, security and security-related dilemmas posed by the Islamic world to the West and by the West to the Islamic world will be a major source of friction. Second, the deterioration of economic and political conditions in many Muslim states will lend greater authority and power to Islamist movements. Third, as the Middle East and other regions experience accelerated political and economic change in the next decade, the strains of change will, at least in the short term, increase the appeal of Islamic groups in many states.

As Western-inspired norms concerning democracy, human rights, free market capitalism, and the primacy of the nation-state encounter resistance, at least in the short to medium term, in troubled regions of the world, there may well be increased demands for solidarity based on the rejection of Western values and the international order organized around them. Radical Islam is likely to be a prominent participant in and beneficiary of a broader movement of this kind.

There is a considerable likelihood that relations between the West and various countries in the Islamic world will in some respects and to varying degrees in different states grow worse before they grow better. Based on historical experience Muslim regimes are more likely than most other Third World regimes to pursue policies that might eventually lead to Western action against them, such as economic sanctions, breaking of diplomatic relations, or even military action. Muslim societies have historically been highly sensitive to the need to preserve the honor and integrity of their culture, sensitive to external slights and pressures, and more inclined to break off diplomatic relations with offending states. (Historically the Arab-Israeli conflict has been the key source of these ruptures; its significance should diminish with dramatic progress.)

Muslim culture is perhaps more inclined than most to believe that it can and will "abide" for long periods under severe international hardships rather than compromising the integrity of its position and culture. To the West this represents fanaticism and inflexibility and an unwillingness to face the "reality" of unequal power relationships. In Muslim political and strategic culture it is understood as a refusal to compromise dignity and sovereignty in the face of superior power. Martyrdom, furthermore, is more regularly integrated into the political vocabulary of Islam than in most other political cultures. This characteristic tends to make Muslim societies in general and Islamist regimes in particular less flexible in their dealings with the West and regional competitors, especially if compromise is seen as the required outcome of unequal power relationships.

The Rise of Political Islam

The role of Islam is likely to grow in the internal politics of Muslim countries. Islamic politics will serve to revolutionize the old orders and elite structures that have been founded on minority power and authoritarian or despotic means of control. The spread of democracy to the region will initially have much the same destabilizing impact, independent of Islam. In fact, because of political Islam's threat to existing regimes and the status quo, many Muslim regimes are showing growing hostility to these movements and a determination to suppress them. The West's problem may thus be more with *movements* than with regimes—until Islamists come to power. But it would be dangerous for Western policy makers to conclude that the crushing of these movements by the state represents a solution; in most cases it does not. These movements reflect deep-seated political, economic, and societal problems; repressed and underground, Islamic movements in turn tend to be viewed by much of the Muslim public as the only answer to their societies' predicaments. Under these circumstances, and in many settings, Islamist movements are acquiring a monopoly by default as the only serious opposition to failing regimes.

In our view the basic conflict is not between Islam and non-Islam but between ideas and movements and counterideas and countermovements within the same Islamic culture. In its dealings with the West, Islam in political terms can often be understood as the functional equivalent of nationalism, not necessarily a negative force in itself but potentially subject to the same kinds of extremism and prickly sensitivity to external pressures and slights. In its political agenda Islam devotes major attention to the moral basis of societal relationships. Its prescriptions for social, political, and economic problems lie essentially in strengthening the moral environment of society— a worthy goal in itself. Islamic politics do not, however, represent a coherent body of policies waiting to be implemented; rather, they are a vision about the character of history and the world, and a series of attitudes about how politics should be conducted. Otherwise, like nationalism, political Islam generally lacks any inherent, specific, concrete political agenda that offers concrete solutions to concrete problems beyond vague references to greater application of Islamic law.

Few Islamic movements on the horizon appear capable of modernizing Islamic principles sufficiently to make Islamic law more broadly compatible with international legal norms, human and minority rights, and the body of secular law in various societies. Without the ability to compromise, Islamist regimes are unlikely to meet the challenge of change and modernization in ways that will enable them to function successfully in the modern world. Their failure will only intensify frustration and resentment of the West and the international order.

Political Islam, however, is neither static nor blindly seeking to turn back the political clock. On the contrary, it is evolving, gaining experience and maturity, developing greater awareness of political realities, and greater understanding of Western political institutions, political theory, and procedure, and even many key concepts of democratic practice. There is an increasingly wide spectrum of political views and tactics among Islamists, ranging from democratic modernizers to radical activists advocating violence, to reactionaries who have no coherent vision for the future. It is the exclusion of political Islam from any part of the political process that intensifies its most radical and polarizing features. By contrast, its inclusion in the political system tends to encourage its more rapid evolution, moderation, and engagement with contemporary needs.

It is a reality of politics in the contemporary Muslim world that Islamic organizations are the most likely and effective source of opposition to existing regimes, generally enjoying greater legitimacy in the public eye and having deeper grass-roots support than other parties. Unless political systems are open to a variety of competing forces, the Islamists are the most likely inheritors of power when authoritarian regimes break down.

Because the phenomenon of political Islam is being mishandled by a number of important states such as Egypt and Algeria, the chances of Islamists coming to power in one or both states in the next several years are considerable. Over the long run states such as Uzbekistan, Syria, Tunisia, Libya, or Morocco could also face a serious Islamist challenge. The West Bank and Gaza too, are at considerable risk, but a genuine and successful Palestinian-Israeli accord will almost surely reduce the radical threat. New Islamist regimes would not necessarily have to resemble Iran in terms of internal or external politics, although the only case of a Sunni Islamist regime to date, in Sudan, offers little encouragement for good governance and regional order springing from an Islamic movement.

Islam and the West in the International System

In the new post–Cold War strategic environment there are ever-growing arenas in which Islam and the West are destined to interact, for better or for worse. Additionally, with the relaxation of global discipline and new international freedom of action after the Cold War, elements in both the West and the Islamic world are increasingly inclined to resuscitate old but enduring images derived from the 1,000-year experience of confrontation and coexistence between Islam and the West—the original "Cold War." These images are useful to extremists on both sides to justify xenophobic policies. Indeed, Muslims today feel under siege: they are victims of Western military action (Iraq, Libya, Lebanon, Iran), they face Israeli military action (the Occupied

Territories, Lebanon, Egypt, Syria, Jordan, Tunisia, Iraq), they are losing sectarian wars with Christian populations (Bosnia, Azerbaijan, Russia), they are losing conflicts with Hindu sectarianism (India, Kashmir). In addition, Muslims now feel they are victimized by a concerted international effort to discredit Islam and to blacken the name of Muslims everywhere. Even Muslims living in the West feel they are objects of surveillance and even harassment from the public whenever a Muslim-inspired terrorist incident occurs anywhere in the West. Muslim paranoia is growing.

Similarly, negative images are heightened in the West, where Western citizens and societies are objects of sporadic Muslim attack, including bombings, assassination, hijacking, and kidnapping by Islamist terrorists. Whereas international terrorism may make the West feel it is under Muslim siege based on a few spectacular incidents, Muslim society, by contrast, feels itself profoundly at odds with the international scene. This mutual sense of siege is dangerous and a classic prerequisite for a blind march toward armed conflict.

It may be only a small handful of spectacular issues, such as the bombing of the World Trade Center, that will prove decisive in grabbing the headlines and the minds of the public and policy makers and in determining the attitude taken toward the broader, much more complex, but ultimately manageable Islamist phenomenon as a whole. Declaratory U.S. policy rightly does not seek to declare war on Islam, or even Islamism, so much as to confront unacceptable acts by Muslim groups or states that violate international norms.

It is a central conclusion of this book that frictions between Islam and the West are likely to interact with broader cleavages along North-South lines, between haves and have-nots. As the nonaligned movement loses its relevance, political Islam has emerged as a major ideological force in the Third World. In the future, the foreign and security policy agendas of the Islamic world and the south may seem to converge, at least from a Western perspective. Indeed, Islam could serve as a rallying cry of the economic have-nots across the Muslim world against what is seen as Western domination of the post–Cold War economic and political order. The linkage of radical Islam with other ideologies that challenge the prevailing international order is a distinct possibility despite the lack of a strong redistributive tradition within Islam.

The Strategic Dimension

The friction between Islam and the West manifests itself largely along *functional* rather than geographic lines. Under adverse circumstances a wide range of bilateral problems can become aggregated and consolidated to the point of taking on the broader character of "cultural or religious struggle" in the eyes of extremists. At that point the concrete issues become harder to deal with because they become garbed in ideological mantles, masking negotiable and manageable solutions.

Political Islam will certainly seek to enhance the real power of Islamic states in order to minimize their inherent weakness in dealing with the West as well as neighboring states. This goal may well imply a search for greater military power, even including the acquisition of nuclear weapons and the means for their delivery in order to put relations with the West on a more equal footing. These goals are not unique to Islamist politicians. They are widely shared by nationalist leaders across the Third World who wish to avoid dealing with the West from a position of strategic weakness. Moreover, Islamist political groups and personalities vary widely. There is no reason to assume an Islamist government will pursue a blind search for military power as its utmost priority; the goal of national strength will compete with many other pressing domestic objectives. In the end, and without dismissing the havoc that zealotry can bring to the international system, Islamic leaders will have to deal from a position of realism about the way the world works, including the tendency of assertive postures to provoke equally assertive strategies of containment.

Islam is a central issue in many of the most explosive national and ethnic conflicts worldwide, where Muslim communities and Muslim states are important actors: Bosnia, the West Bank and Gaza, Cyprus, Kashmir, Azerbaijan-Armenia, and southern Sudan among the most prominent. The post–Cold War reassertion of nationalist and radical Islamist aspirations share many of the same roots. The issue of Western intervention in these areas will be central to the evolution of Muslim foreign policy and the evolution of relations between Islam and the West.

Religious and cultural fault lines between Islam and the West exist from East Asia across Central Asia, the Caucasus, the Balkans, and the Mediterranean. These are potentially some of the greatest areas for immediate political/cultural friction. Cultural fault lines may be most intense between Islam and Eastern Orthodox Christianity, rather than with Western (Roman Catholic, Protestant) Christian communities, given the intimate linkages between Orthodox churches and local nationalisms.

Instability within the Muslim world itself and the insecure character of Islamic societies will also pose a challenge to the international order. Muslim societies face formidable internal and external security challenges, with a corresponding traditional reliance on the utility of force in inter and intrastate relations. (This characteristic, again, is not unique to the Muslim world but is common to much of the Third World, where mechanisms for conflict resolution short of the use of force are lacking.) Many of these internal and external challenges in the Muslim world flow from the pressing need for political and social change. Far from posing unique threats to the West, most of the hard security risks addressed in this book are the result of local or regional conditions, oriented along Muslim-Muslim or South-South lines. But Europe and the United States will nonetheless be exposed to the systemic and spillover effects of competition, conflict, and change within the Muslim world, from refugee flows to pressures for international intervention in crisis situations.

In this context, the growth of arsenals is rightly a leading part of Western concern. The proliferation of conventional and unconventional weapons across the Muslim world, driven largely by regional rivalries, poses a growing risk to Muslim states themselves as well as to Europe, and by extension, to the United States. The acquisition of weapons of mass destruction and the means for their delivery at longer ranges has emerged as a leading symbol and instrument of the drive for geostrategic weight among regional powers in the post–Cold War world. At the same time, conventional arsenals in the South have likewise grown, unconstrained by the arms control limitations in place on the European continent. Muslim states themselves are the most likely first targets when all these weapons are used. The increasing exposure and vulnerability of Europe (and U.S. military facilities and forces in and around Europe) to the weapons of nearby Muslim countries will reinforce the lesson, already apparent during the Gulf War, that Mediterranean and European security cannot be insulated from the consequences of developments in the greater Muslim world.

In the realm of economic security, the West realistically cannot dismiss the possible use of the "oil weapon," as well as control of important pipelines and sea-lanes, as key instruments of Islamist foreign policy in the future. Although no Middle Eastern leader hostile to the West (Qadhafi, Saddam Hussein, Khomeini) has invoked the oil weapon in the past, the use of oil embargo by Saudi Arabia in 1973 made this contingency a permanent concern in Western strategic thought from the mid-1960s through the mid-1980s. Western strategists thus take note that the confluence of two trends, the rise of Islamic politics and the possible tightening of the world oil market in the late 1990s, could offer new opportunities for the political use of oil by an unfriendly regime under adverse circumstances. If the only power that Muslim states possess vis-à-vis the West is economic, it would be surprising if they were not tempted to use it in some fashion as a balancing factor against overwhelming Western political and military power.

Indeed, even friendly oil states might not hesitate to suggest that modest "political" adjustments in oil prices and supply are as natural an instrument of persuasion for Muslim states to use as are the threatened or actual use of economic sanctions by the West. Similarly, should an Islamist regime or a regime loath to offend Islamist political sensibilities come to power in Cairo, Western confidence in access to the Suez Canal for the purposes of supporting a future intervention in the Gulf must decline. The likelihood or effectiveness of these tactics by Islamist regimes is an open question, but even their possible use has powerful political impact, especially as the West comes to realize that its ability to regularly and easily impose its strategic will is growing more difficult in the new world environment.

Islam will inevitably be invoked in the practice of international political violence or "terrorism" by extremist groups. In fact, radical Islamic groups have been among the most lethal in international terrorism, and a number of Muslim states have been central to the phenomenon of state sponsorship. Regrettably, Western perceptions of Islam are perhaps unjustifiably shaped by the association of religion with political violence. Nonetheless, the terrorist dimension will remain significant in shaping the future character of relations between Islam and the West. One regrettable consequence of an otherwise successful Arab-Israeli settlement might be the prospects for radical groups' bringing their battles to Western societies in an effort to block a settlement. An outcome of the conflict in the former Yugoslavia, which leaves large numbers of displaced and persecuted Bosnian Muslims seemingly abandoned by the West, could spawn another movement on the Palestinian model, with serious implications for international political violence.

Democracy and Human Rights

The rise of political Islam will pose a continuing dilemma for policy makers concerned with the promotion of democracy and human rights. The experience in Algeria has raised in the minds of many the question of the compatibility of Islamic rule and the practice of democracy as understood in the West. Although there is probably nothing inherently incompatible between Muslim society and democracy, the antidemocratic statements of some radical Islamist leaders have not been reassuring to Western policy makers. Indeed, many secular (and often authoritarian) regimes across the Middle East have themselves been most active in calling attention to the "Islamic threat" in geopolitical terms, emphasizing the destabilizing role of Iran and

Sudan. Yet despite Western concerns over "fundamentalism," it is significant to note that American and European observers are often as inclined to interpret the clash with political Islam in Egypt, Algeria, and elsewhere as a human rights problem every bit as much as a security problem.

Islam in the West

The issue is no longer just Islam and the West but, rather, Islam *in* the West. Many of the most pressing issues for relations between Islam and the West relate to societal issues within the West itself rather than to interstate relations. The growing demographic imbalance between a prosperous North and a poor South has produced powerful migration pressures and equally powerful problems of integration and social cohesion. Violence against large and well-established Muslim communities is a leading agent of instability in the new Europe and has had a negative effect on wider relations between Islam and the West. The fate of Bosnia's Muslims—inside Europe—and perceived Western indifference or inaction have had a marked effect on attitudes toward the United States and Europe in even the most moderate secular quarters in the Muslim world. The perception that after the Cold War Europe is now intent on erecting a new Iron Curtain along North-South or civilizational lines is widespread and has begun to affect political and strategic debates from Rabat to Jakarta.

Policy Implications

Political and Economic

The Muslim world is almost certain to witness the accession to power of one or more new Islamist governments over the next decade, most likely in the Arab world. States most susceptible to the rise of Islamist power seem to be those

- where population growth is high and the needs of large urbanized communities go unmet;
- where low standards of living are intensified by the appearance of pervasive corruption;
- where governments have eliminated most meaningful political opposition and the Islamists therefore have no rivals;
- where governments have used major force to crush the strength of the Islamists, thereby only polarizing and exacerbating the problem; and

- where the Islamists have come to assume the role of sole legitimate opposition force in the opinion of the people.

This pattern fits the case of Iran, and it resembles the developing situations in Egypt and Algeria. Uzbekistan represents another longer-term possibility. Afghanistan, also, as part of the legacy of the anti-Soviet struggle, could fall into the hands of hard-line Islamists through the power of the gun. Situations in which Islamists come to power by coup, as in Sudan, are less predictable, with deteriorating social environments offering only limited warning signs of the growth of Islamist power.

United States policy options are quite limited in terms of forestalling eventual takeover of Islamist movements. Clearly the negative power of social despair indicates that improvement of internal conditions is a key goal, but can outside powers readily change the features of an ineffective and unjust economic and social system? The most the United States can do is to spot negative political, economic, and social trends and warn the regimes in question of U.S. concern, and perhaps of U.S. inability to assist more meaningfully unless reforms are undertaken. These policy approaches can in all likelihood have no more than minor effect against a backdrop of pervasive malaise in declining regimes, but the warnings must be issued, at least in private. At the same time, dialogue with moderate Islamic groups is worth pursuing. A viable approach to the stable evolution of the Muslim world will require an open dialogue with legitimate opposition as well as governing forces. This will be essential to developing a *modus vivendi* with groups whose external policies are largely unformed. The need for dialogue is all the more urgent, since Western policies aimed at marginalizing radical Islamic movements through economic development are unlikely to alter patterns of opposition within a politically relevant time frame. Because political reform may lead to faster results, hard-pressed regimes should be encouraged to bring nonviolent Islamist groups into the political process.

Where Islamists come to power, the United States should be able to state the minimum conditions necessary for useful bilateral relations. Most of these conditions will relate to international norms of conduct and human rights. Strict domestic social and moral restrictions if evenly and legally applied may not be attractive by Western standards, but they may not in themselves be grounds for confrontation except where they clearly violate human rights. Respect for international norms and law should be the primary criteria by which the acceptability of a given regime is measured.

No clear-cut policies that will clearly forestall an ideological confrontation between "Islam and the West" can be prescribed for the United States and its international partners. There are, nonetheless, some suggestions that might lessen the risk of a broader friction along these lines. The principal challenge for the West is to ensure that a whole range of individual bilateral and multi-lateral problems are not allowed to gather into a broader cultural confronta-tion with Islam. In practice this means that grievances against Muslim coun-tries should not be framed with reference to Islam unless Islam as an ideolo-gy is a specific part of the problem. It is desirable to avoid criticism of radical Islam in terms that are directed at the religion itself or refer vaguely to "dan-gers of Islamic fundamentalism." Such efforts only have the effect of high-lighting the ideological dimension. Concrete grievances should be delivered in precise, functional terms: communal violence, violation of human rights, bigotry, antidemocratic procedures, advocacy of policies harmful to U.S. inter-ests or the interests of the international system, acts of terrorism and violence, and support for violent conspiracies within Western societies. These objec-tions are generic, international in character, and have reference to objection-able actions by any group, regardless of religion or ideology.

Indeed, radical Islam is only strengthened when it is referred to repeatedly and publicly by top officials as a major threat. Charges aimed at "fundamen-talism" demonstrate to would-be adherents that Islamic movements must indeed be very powerful and effective at keeping the West at bay, that "they must be doing something right if it upsets the West to such an extent."

Strategic

To the extent that Western societies can reduce their dependence on oil imports from the Greater Middle East, the role of oil as a flashpoint in rela-tions between the Muslim world and the West will be reduced. The integra-tion of the newly independent and largely Muslim oil-producing states of the Caucasus and Central Asia into the world energy market makes this a more pressing political concern. The diversification of routes for the shipment of oil and gas from the Gulf, the former Soviet Union, and North Africa should be encouraged through appropriate support for new pipeline ventures in the eastern and western Mediterranean. New networks of this sort could have the additional benefit of binding together the economic interests of Muslim and Western countries in unstable regions

Weapons proliferation and growing military capability in the Muslim South may appear to have a strong Muslim-Western presence. But our coun-terproliferation policies cannot and should not be framed in terms of an Islamic threat. Policy makers and strategists must nonetheless begin to address the consequences of an environment in which Western states are more exposed to the retaliatory consequences of our actions in the Muslim world, and in the Third World more generally. Again, it should recognized that Muslim states themselves are most exposed to the effects of the spread of conventional and unconventional weapons, a reality that could eventually foster mutual interest in regional arms control and confidence-building arrangements along key Muslim-Western fault lines.

The rise of Islam as a factor in international relations, particularly along the European periphery, will increase the importance of borderland states in Western strategy and policy. By virtue of their history and location, states on the marches between the Islamic world and the West, including those in southern Europe, will become more central to U.S. and European policy. These states and their counterparts in the Muslim world, such as Morocco, Tunisia, and Turkey, are already emerging as active interlocutors in strategic terms. All of this suggests that supporting the political and economic development of key states in the Muslim world may be at least as important to the future stability of the international system as the reform and integration of the former communist states.

Finally, post–Cold War requirements for international intervention and peacekeeping will necessarily bring the West into closer diplomatic and military contact with the Muslim world. Cooperation with Muslim states will often be a prerequisite for the success of multinational operations. Moreover, if past and present patterns of conflict are any guide, these operations will often be conducted in the Muslim world or where Muslim interests are at stake. Cooperation with moderate Muslim regimes will acquire even greater significance in the context of the United Nation's growing role in peacekeeping and peacemaking.

Perceptions in the Muslim world and the West may betray a sense of mutual siege, as well as the sense that relations have reached a defining moment. It is the task of policy makers and intelligent observers on all sides to explore the bases for a practical *modus vivendi* within an international system that compels interaction and within the increasingly diverse societies of the West.

Selected Bibliography

Articles

Addi, Lahouari. "Islamist Utopia and Democracy." *Annals of the American Academy of Political and Social Science,* November 1992.

Anderson, Lisa. "Obligation and Accountability: Islamic Politics in North Africa." *Daedalus,* Summer 1991.

Ayubi, Nazih N. "State Islam and Communal Plurality." *Annals of the American Academy of Political and Social Science,* November 1992.

Deeb, Mary-Jane. "Militant Islam and the Politics of Redemption." *Annals of the American Academy of Political and Social Science,* November 1992.

Gaffney, Patrick D. "Popular Islam." *Annals of the American Academy of Political and Social Science,* November 1992.

Ghannouchi, Rachid. "Islam and the West: Realities and Prospects." *Inquiry,* March-April 1993.

Gomel, Giorgio. "Migration toward Western Europe: Trends, Outlook, Policies." (Rome) *International Spectator* April-June 1992.

Hadar, Leon T. "What Green Peril?" *Foreign Affairs,* Spring 1993.

Hartley, Anthony. "Europe's Muslims." *The National Interest,* Winter 1990/91.

Huntington, Samuel. "The Clash of Civilizations?" *Foreign Affairs,* Summer 1993.

Karawan, Ibrahim A. "Monarchs, Mullas and Marshalls: Islamic Regimes?" *Annals of the American Academy of Political and Social Science,* November 1992.

Kodmani-Darwish, Bassma. "International Security and the Forces of Nationalism and Fundamentalism." In *New Dimensions in International Security.* Adelphi Paper No. 266 (London: IISS, Winter 1991/92).

Kramer, Martin. "Islam vs. Democracy." *Commentary,* January 1993.

Leveau, Remy. "Maghrebi Immigration to Europe: Double Insertion of Double Exclusion?" *Annals of the American Academy of Political and Social Science,* November 1992.

Lewis, Bernard. "The Roots of Muslim Rage." *Atlantic Monthly,* September 1990.

Loescher, Gil. "Refugee Movements and International Security." *Adelphi Paper* No. 268 (London: IISS, Summer 1992).

Miller, Judith. "The Challenge of Radical Islam." *Foreign Affairs,* Spring 1993.

Naumkin, Vitaly. "International Security and the Forces of Nationalism and Fundamentalism." *New Dimensions in International Security.* Adelphi Paper No. 266 (London: IISS, Winter 1991/92).

Pfaff, William. "Reflections: Islam and the West." *New Yorker,* January 28, 1991.

Prodromou, Elizabeth H. "Toward an Understanding of Eastern Orthodoxy and Democracy Building in the Post–Cold War Balkins." *Mediterranean Quarterly,* Spring 1994.

Roberts, Adam. "Humanitarian War: Military Intervention and Human Rights." *International Affairs* (London), July 1993.

Rubenstein, Alvin Z., and Soliman, Pauline. "America in Egypt's Press." *Mediterranean Quarterly,* Spring 1994.

Salame, Ghassan. "Islam and the West." *Foreign Policy,* Spring 1993.

—   **Books**

Abu Lughod, Janet L. *Before European Hegemony: The World System A.D. 1250–1350.* New York: Oxford University Press, 1989.

Ahmed, Akbar S. *Discovering Islam: Making Sense of Muslim History and Society.* London: Routledge, 1988.

Aliboni, Roberto, ed. *Southern European Security in the 1990s,* London: Pinter, 1992.

Ayoob, Mohammed, ed. *The Politics of Islamic Reassertion.* London: Croom Helm, 1981.

Booth, Ken. *Strategy and Ethnocentrism.* London: Croom Helm, 1979.

Bozeman, Adda B. *Strategic Intelligence and Statecraft: Selected Essays.* Washington, D.C.: Brasseys, 1992.

Braudel, Fernand. *The Mediterranean and the Mediterranean World in the Age of Philip II.* New York: Perennial Library, Harper & Row, 1972.

Burgat, François. *The Islamic Movement in North Africa.* Austin: Center for Middle Eastern Studies, University of Texas, 1993.

Denoeux, Guilain. *Urban Unrest in the Middle East: A Comparative Study of Informal Networks in Egypt, Iran, and Lebanon.* Albany: State University of New York Press, 1993.

Esman, Milton J., and Rabinovich, Itamar, eds. *Ethnicity, Pluralism, and the State in the Middle East,* Ithaca, NY:Cornell University Press, 1988.

Esposito, John L. *The Islamic Threat: Myth or Reality?* New York: Oxford University Press, 1992.

Fuller, Graham E., and Lesser, Ian O., with Henze, Paul B., and Brown, J.F. *Turkey's New Geopolitics: From the Balkans to Western China,* Boulder, CO: Westview Press, 1993.

Gladney, Dru C. *Muslim Chinese: Ethnic Nationalism in the People's Republic.* Cambridge, MA: Harvard University Press, 1991.

Gordon, David C. *Images of the West: Third World Perspectives.* Rowman & Littlefield, Savage, 1989.

Hourani, Albert. *Islam in European Thought.* Cambridge: Cambridge University Press, 1991.

Juergensmeyer, Mark. *The New Cold War?: Religious Nationalism Confronts the Secular State.* Berkeley: University of California Press, 1993.

El-Kenz, Ali. *Algerian Reflections on Arab Crises.* Austin: Center for Middle Eastern Studies, University of Texas Press, 1991.

Kepel, Giles. *Muslim Extremism in Egypt: The Prophet and Pharaoh.* Berkeley: University of California Press, 1985.

Lapidus, Ira M. *A History of Islamic States.* Cambridge: Cambridge University Press, 1988.

Lesser, Ian O. *Security in North Africa: Internal and External Challenges.* Santa Monica, CA: RAND, 1993.

Lewis, Bernard. *The Political Language of Islam.* Chicago: University of Chicago Press, 1988.

Lewis, Bernard. *The Emergence of Modern Turkey.* London: Oxford University Press, 1961.

Lewis, Bernard. *Islam and the West*. New York: Oxford University Press, 1993.

Lewis, Bernard. *The Muslim Discovery of Europe*. New York: W. W. Norton, 1982.

Mayer, Ann Elizabeth, *Islam and Human Rights: Tradition and Politics*. Boulder, CO: Westview Press, 1991.

Mazrui, Ali. *Cultural Forces in World Politics*. Portsmouth, New Hampshire, UK: Heinemann, 1990.

Mernissi, Fatima. *Beyond the Veil*. Bloomington: Indiana University Press, 1975.

Mernissi, Fatima. *Islam and Democracy: Fear of the Modern World*. Menlo Park, CA: Addison-Wesley, 1992.

Mortimer, Edward. *Faith and Power: The Politics of Islam*. New York: Random House, 1982.

Parry, V. J., and Yapp, M. E., eds., *War, Technology and Society in the Middle East*. London: Oxford University Press, 1975.

Pirenne, Henri. *Mohammed and Charlemagne*. London: Unwin University Books, 1974; first published 1939.

Ramazani, R. K. *Revolutionary Iran*. Baltimore: Johns Hopkins University Press, 1988.

Said, Edward. *Orientalism*. New York: Random House, 1978.

Said, Edward. *Culture and Imperialism*. New York: Knopf, 1993.

Sisk, Timothy D. *Islam and Democracy: Religion, Politics and Power in the Middle East*. Washington, D.C.: U.S. Institute of Peace, 1992.

Sivan, Emmanuel. *Radical Islam: Medieval Theology and Modern Politics*. New Haven: Yale University Press, 1985.

Smith, William Cantwell. *Islam in Modern History*. Princeton, N.J.: Princeton University Press, 1957.

Smock, David R. *Religious Perspectives on War: Christian, Muslim and Jewish Attitudes toward Force after the Gulf War*. Washington, D.C.: U.S. Institute of Peace, 1992.

Spencer, Claire. *The Maghreb in the 1990s*. Adelphi Paper No. 274. London: IISS, 1993.

Tibi, Bassam. *Islam and the Cultural Accommodation of Social Change*. Boulder CO: Westview Press, 1991.

Vasconcelos, Alvaro, ed. *Européens et Maghrébins: Une Solidarité Obligée*. Paris: Karthala, 1993.

Zakarya, Rafiq. *The Struggle Within Islam*. New York: Penguin, 1989.

Zartman, I. William, and Habeeb, William Mark. *Polity and Society in Contemporary North Africa*. Boulder, CO: Westview Press, 1993.

About the Authors

Graham E. Fuller is a Senior Political Scientist at RAND. He served 20 years as a foreign service officer, including three years in Istanbul, and was the National Intelligence Officer for long-range Middle East forecasting at the CIA. His degrees include a B.A. and an M.A. from Harvard University. Mr. Fuller speaks fluent Turkish and Russian. He recently finished a study on modern Turkey entitled *Turkey's New Geopolitics: From the Balkans to Western China* (Westview Press). Among his other publications are RAND studies on Islamic fundamentalism in Turkey, Iran, Afghanistan, and Pakistan. He is also the author of two books: *The "Center of the Universe": The Geopolitics of Iran* (Westview, 1991), and *The Democracy Trap: Perils of the Post-Cold War World* (Dutton, 1992).

Ian O. Lesser is a senior member of the International Policy Department at RAND, specializing in European and Mediterranean affairs. Prior to joining RAND, he was a Senior Fellow in International Security Affairs at the Center for Strategic and International Studies, and has also been a Senior Fellow of the Atlantic Council and a staff consultant at International Energy Associates in Washington D.C. A graduate of the University of Pennsylvania, the London School of Economics, and the Fletcher School of Law and Diplomacy, he received his doctorate from St. Antony's College, Oxford. Dr. Lesser is the author of *Resources and Strategy* (St. Martin's Press, 1989), and *Turkey's New Geopolitics: From the Balkans to Western China* (Westview Press), as well as numerous publications on southern European countries and the Mediterranean affairs.

About the Book

"The clash of civilizations" has become a common phrase in discussions of U.S.–Middle East relations. This book explores the nature of the friction between the Muslim world and Western states, looking at legitimate perceptions and grievances on both sides involving historical, political, economic, cultural, psychological, and strategic elements.

Arguing that "Islam versus the West" does not represent the arena of the next global ideological struggle, the authors examine specific issues of a bilateral nature that require careful handling to prevent the consolidation of states into opposing blocs. They discuss Islam's efforts to politically enhance the real power of Muslim states and to equalize relations with the West in the strategic arena; the enlarged role of Islam in the internal politics of Muslim countries; and the urgency of political, economic, and social change to break away from traditional authoritarian orders. A central theme of the book is that political Islam threatens the established order in most Muslim countries far more than it threatens the West and that violent confrontation can best be circumvented by integrating Islamist forces into the political process.

Index

188

INDEX

Israel
  Arab dispute, 21, 164
  Arab peace, 86
  Declaration of Principles, 87
  establishment of, 39
  PLO Accord, 128
  West Bank elections, 134
  as Western outpost, 40
  Zionism, 40
Istanbul, 135, *see also* Constantinople
Italy, 34, 71, 73, 74

J
Jakarta, 171
Jerusalem, Christian, 30
Jesus, prophet, 29
Jewish, Palestine, state in, 30
Jews, 3
Jihad
  Christian, 31
  Islamic, Palestine Liberation
      Front, 73
  propagation of faith, 9
  purification and preservation of
      Islam, 102
  as religious obligation, 101
  Soviets in Afghanistan, 22
  Spanish expulsion, 17
  trends in United States, 92
Jordan, 35

K
Kahane, Rabbi Meir, 107
Kashmir, 43, 160, 168
Kausikan, Bilahari, 127
Kazakhstan, 65, 68, 70
Khadhafi, Mu'ammar al-, *see*
      Qadhafi, Mu'ammar al-
Khartoum, 128

Khomeini, Ayatollah, 2, 43, 102, 127,
      169
Kissinger, Henry, 83
Kokand, Uzbekistan, 12
Koran, *see* Quran
Korea, peninsula, stability in, 66
Kuk, Rabbi Avraham Yitzhak, 107
Kurdish Workers Party, 52
Kurds, 41, 52, 114
Kuwait, 41, 61, 83, 95, 160
  United States invasion, 84

L
Lampedusa, 67
League of Nations, 37
Lebanon, 41, 74, 128, 160, 166
Legal system, dual, 101
Lesser, Ian O., 10
Levy, Bernard-Henri, 55
Libya, 41, 61, 65, 66, 67, 69, 72, 73, 155,
      166

M
Maghreb, export of labor, 87
Mahathir, Prime Minister, Malaysia,
      127, 147
Malaysia, 56, 137
Marca, Islam borderlands, 157
Marxism, 128
Mazrui, Ali, 34
Mecca, 32
Mediterranean
  colonialism, 138
  common civilization, 15
  as Muslim sea, 31
  treaty, Algerian revolution, 25
Melilla, 62
Mexico, 70
Middle East, Common Market, 87